# A Case for the Divinity of Jesus

Dr. Maxwell Shimba

Printed by Shimba Publishing LLC
Printed in the United States of America

# TABLE OF CONTENTS

*A Case for the Divinity of Jesus*

# INTRODUCTION

A Case for the Divinity of Jesus

The question of Jesus's divinity has been at the heart of theological debates for centuries. From the earliest days of Christianity, the Church has affirmed that Jesus is not merely a wise teacher, prophet, or enlightened individual, but rather the incarnate Son of God—fully divine, co-equal with the Father, and worthy of worship. The belief in the divinity of Christ is foundational to Christian faith. However, in our contemporary world, this doctrine has been challenged by skeptics, liberal theologians, and even some within Christian circles who question the traditional understanding of who Jesus truly is.

In this book, A Case for the Divinity of Jesus, we explore the biblical, theological, and historical evidence that affirms Jesus as God in the flesh. The aim of this work is to demonstrate that the doctrine of Christ's divinity is not only supported by Scripture but is also essential for the understanding of salvation, the nature of God, and the Christian faith itself.

Dr. Maxwell Shimba, in this thorough and well-researched treatise, brings together expository analysis, comprehensive commentary, and exhaustive references from both the Old and New Testaments. Through a combination of scriptural exegesis, Strong's Concordance analysis, and a deep dive into historical and theological contexts, this book builds a strong case for the belief that Jesus is God—the second person of the Trinity, eternally existing and unchanging.

As you journey through the chapters of this book, you will encounter familiar passages and discover new insights that reveal the profound truth that Jesus Christ is YHWH, the Lord Almighty. This truth is not merely academic; it has deep implications for our lives, our faith, and our relationship with God. The divinity of Jesus is the cornerstone upon which the entire structure of Christianity rests.

The Alpha and Omega – Jesus as the Eternal God

Revelation introduces us to one of the most profound titles attributed to both God and Jesus: "I am the Alpha and the Omega," a declaration of eternity, sovereignty, and divine power. This title, found in both Revelation 1:8 and Revelation 22:13, speaks of God's eternal nature, being the beginning and the end, the source and completion of all things. The Alpha (the first letter of the Greek alphabet) and Omega (the last letter) symbolize the all-encompassing nature of God, from creation to consummation. What makes this title particularly significant is that it is applied not only to God the Father but also to Jesus Christ.

- Revelation 1:8: "I am the Alpha and the Omega, the beginning and the end, says the Lord God, who is, who was, and who is to come, the Almighty."

- Revelation 22:13-16: "I am the Alpha and the Omega, the first and the last, the beginning and the end… I, Jesus, have sent my angel to give you this testimony for the churches."

These passages draw a direct parallel between Jesus and God in terms of their eternal nature. If YHWH (the LORD Almighty) is the Alpha and Omega, and Jesus claims the same title, then it is clear that Jesus is identifying Himself with YHWH, the eternal God.

The Divine Identity of Jesus

In Revelation, we find Jesus speaking in the same authoritative terms as God Himself, emphasizing His eternality and sovereign lordship over all things. This title, Alpha and Omega, is used to signify eternal existence—the One who was there at the beginning and will be there at the end. Jesus, therefore, is not a created being, nor is He a secondary deity. He is co-eternal with the Father, fully participating in the divine identity.

The phrase "who is, who was, and who is to come" (Revelation 1:8) also echoes the language used by YHWH in the Old Testament. In Exodus 3:14, when God reveals Himself to Moses at the burning bush, He says, "I AM THAT I AM." This declaration of God's eternal being is reflected in the description of Jesus in Revelation as the One who exists in all ages—past, present, and future.

The eternal nature of Jesus is further affirmed by His resurrection from the dead, making Him the "firstborn from the dead" (Revelation 1:5) and the "living one" who holds "the keys of death and Hades" (Revelation 1:18). By overcoming death, Jesus has demonstrated His power over life and death, a power that only God possesses.

Strong's Concordance Analysis

- Alpha (ἄλφα, Alpha, Strong's G1): The first letter of the Greek alphabet, symbolizing the beginning.

- Omega (Ὦ, Omega, Strong's G5598): The last letter of the Greek alphabet, symbolizing the end or completion.

- Almighty (παντοκράτωρ, Pantokratōr, Strong's G3841): Referring to God's absolute power and authority over all creation.

These terms underscore the divine authority of Jesus. He is the origin of all things and their destiny—both creator and consummator of history.

Jesus as the "First and the Last"

The title "First and the Last" is another significant phrase applied to both YHWH and Jesus in the Scriptures. In Isaiah 44:6, YHWH says, "I am the first, and I am the last; besides me, there is no God." This statement is an assertion of God's uniqueness—His absolute sovereignty and authority as the one true God.

In the New Testament, Jesus appropriates this same title for Himself in Revelation 1:17-18:

- Revelation 1:17-18: "Fear not, I am the first and the last, and the living one. I died, and behold I am alive forevermore, and I have the keys of Death and Hades."

Jesus claims to be the first and the last, a clear indication of His divine status. The repetition of this title in Revelation 2:8 and 22:13 reinforces the identification of Jesus with YHWH, the eternal Lord of all.

This connection is not accidental. The Apostle John, writing under the inspiration of the Holy Spirit, intentionally applies titles reserved for God to Jesus, thereby affirming that

Jesus is not merely a human teacher or an angelic being but God Himself in human flesh.

The Doctrine of Christ's Divinity in Early Christianity

The early Church was built on the understanding that Jesus is God. The Apostles and early Christian leaders consistently taught that Jesus was both fully human and fully divine. This belief is reflected in the Nicene Creed, which affirms that Jesus is "God from God, Light from Light, true God from true God, begotten, not made, of one being with the Father." This confession was based on the teachings of the New Testament and the experiences of the apostles, who witnessed Jesus's resurrection and recognized Him as Lord and God.

The Eternal Sovereignty of Jesus

The titles Alpha and Omega and First and Last affirm that Jesus is eternal, sovereign, and equal with the Father in power and glory. He is the beginning of all things and the end toward which all creation moves. His resurrection demonstrates His victory over death, and His authority over life and death confirms His divine identity.

The acknowledgment of Jesus as God is not an optional belief but a foundational truth of the Christian faith. To deny the divinity of Christ is to misunderstand the nature of God and the work of salvation. As we continue through this book, we will explore more biblical and theological evidence for the divinity of Jesus, affirming that He is truly the Lord Almighty, worthy of our worship and devotion.

# DR. MAXWELL SHIMBA

CHAPTER 01

---

# THE WORD AND THE DIVINE NATURE

*The Word and the Divine Nature – A Comprehensive Exposition of John 1:1*

Introduction: The Mystery of the Word

The opening verse of the Gospel of John sets the stage for one of the most profound theological assertions in the New Testament:

"In the beginning was the Word, and the Word was with God, and the Word was God" (John 1:1, KJV).

This verse introduces us to the concept of the "Word" (Greek: Logos), which holds a dual identity: distinct from God in relationship, yet fully God in essence. The implications of this statement are immense, shaping the Christian understanding of Christ's divinity, the nature of God's self-revelation, and the concept of the Trinity.

The Logos: Defining the Term

The term "Word" in the original Greek is Logos (Strong's G3056), a word rich in meaning. It conveys more than just spoken language; it refers to reason, wisdom, and the divine principle by which God creates and governs the universe. In Hellenistic philosophy, Logos was understood as the rational principle that permeated all things. However, John's use of Logos carries deeper, more theological significance.

In the context of John 1:1, Logos refers to the preexistent Christ. John declares that before time itself, the Logos existed. The Logos was not only present at creation but was intimately involved in it. This is confirmed in John 1:3, which states, "All things were made by him; and without him was not anything made that was made."

"In the Beginning Was the Word"

The phrase "in the beginning" (en archē – Strong's G746) echoes Genesis 1:1, where the Bible says, "In the beginning, God created the heavens and the earth." By using this phrase, John links the activity of the Logos with the creation account, underscoring the eternal existence of the Word. Before anything came into existence, the Logos already "was" (ēn – Strong's G2258), implying timelessness and eternal being. This shows that the Logos transcends time and has always existed as part of God's eternal nature.

"The Word Was With God"

The next part of the verse, "the Word was with God" (pros ton theon – Strong's G4314), indicates a close, intimate relationship between the Logos and God the Father. The preposition pros suggest not merely coexistence but a face-to-face relationship, one of communion and fellowship. This shows a distinction in personhood, laying the foundation for later Trinitarian theology.

The phrase emphasizes that the Logos was not an abstract force or concept but a distinct person, existing alongside the Father. This relationship is reflected in passages such as Proverbs 8:30-31, which speaks of Wisdom being present with God during creation, rejoicing in His works. The Logos is both distinct from God and yet sharing in the divine identity.

## "The Word Was God"

Finally, John declares, "the Word was God" (theos ēn ho logos – Strong's G2316). This statement is unequivocal in asserting the divinity of the Logos. Here, John makes a monumental claim: the Logos is not merely a divine being or godlike figure but is fully and completely God.

Some scholars have noted the absence of the definite article in the Greek phrase (i.e., it says "theos" rather than "ho theos"). This grammatical structure indicates that while the

Logos is fully divine, He is not the same person as the Father. This distinction without separation is key to understanding the doctrine of the Trinity.

Strong's Concordance Analysis

Let us break down the key Greek terms in this verse:

- Word (Logos – Strong's G3056): As mentioned earlier, Logos can mean word, reason, or principle. In John's Gospel, it refers specifically to the preexistent Christ.

- With (pros – Strong's G4314): This preposition indicates close proximity or relationship. It is often used to denote interaction between persons, reinforcing the idea of personal relationship within the Godhead.

- God (Theos – Strong's G2316): The Greek term for God, used here to refer to the divine nature of the Logos. The lack of the definite article in this instance shows that the Logos shares in the divine essence but is not identical in person to God the Father.

Biblical Commentary on John 1:1

The threefold structure of John 1:1 reveals the unity and distinction within the Godhead:

1. "In the beginning was the Word": This highlights the eternal existence of the Logos, transcending time and space.

2. "The Word was with God": Here, we see the personal relationship between the Logos and God the Father, emphasizing their distinct personhood.

3. "The Word was God": This final clause affirms the full divinity of the Logos, declaring that Christ, as the Word, is fully and completely God.

Theological Significance of John 1:1

John 1:1 is foundational to Christian theology for several reasons:

1. Christ's Preexistence: The verse clearly teaches that Christ existed before creation. This is supported by other passages like Colossians 1:17: "He is before all things, and in him all things hold together."

2. Christ's Divinity: John affirms that the Logos is fully God, not a created being or a subordinate deity. This counters later heresies, such as Arianism, which denied the full divinity of Christ.

3. The Doctrine of the Trinity: John 1:1 lays the groundwork for understanding the Trinity. The Logos is distinct from the Father yet one in essence with Him. This mystery is echoed in John 10:30, where Jesus says, "I and the Father are one."

Additional Bible Verses Supporting John 1:1

To fully understand John 1:1, we can examine other scriptures that speak of the relationship between the Father and the Son, and the nature of the Logos:

- John 1:14: "And the Word became flesh and dwelt among us." This verse speaks to the incarnation of the Logos, emphasizing that Jesus is the Word who took on human form.

- Hebrews 1:3: "He is the radiance of the glory of God and the exact imprint of his nature." This passage underscores that Jesus perfectly reflects the nature of God.

- Philippians 2:6-7: "Though he was in the form of God, did not count equality with God a thing to be grasped, but emptied himself." Here we see Christ's divine nature and his willing condescension in the incarnation.

The Word as God and the Source of Life

John 1:1 not only opens the door to a deeper understanding of Christ's nature but also invites us to contemplate the mystery of the Godhead. The Logos—Jesus Christ—is both distinct from the Father and yet fully God, eternal, uncreated, and involved in all aspects of creation. This verse challenges us to recognize the centrality of Christ in God's self-revelation, the creation of the world, and the redemption of humanity.

Understanding John 1:1 is essential for comprehending the nature of the Triune God and the person of Jesus Christ. Through this verse, we are invited to marvel at the mystery of the Logos—the Word who was, is, and forever will be God.

CHAPTER 02

---

# THE DEPENDENCE OF CHRIST ON THE FATHER

*The Dependence of Christ on the Father – An Expository Study of John 5:30*

John 5:30 states, "I can of mine own self do nothing: as I hear, I judge: and my judgment is just; because I seek not mine own will, but the will of the Father which hath sent me." In this verse, Jesus speaks about His dependence on the Father in all He does, revealing the unity of will and purpose between the Son and the Father. This statement invites us into a deeper understanding of the relationship between Jesus and God the Father, particularly how Jesus' mission on earth is perfectly aligned with the Father's will.

Context of John 5:30

To understand the meaning of John 5:30, we must first look at the broader context of John 5. In this chapter, Jesus performs the healing of a man at the pool of Bethesda on the Sabbath, an event that sparks controversy with the Jewish authorities. In response to their objections, Jesus delivers a discourse about His authority, revealing His unique relationship with God the Father. This discourse addresses themes of life, judgment, and resurrection, emphasizing that all of Jesus' works are rooted in the will of the Father.

"I Can of Mine Own Self Do Nothing"

The phrase "I can of mine own self do nothing" (ou dynamai poiein ap' emautou ouden – Strong's G1410, G1683, G3762) expresses Jesus' complete reliance on the Father in all His actions. The Greek word for "can" is dynamai (Strong's G1410), meaning "to be able" or "to have power." Here, Jesus is not saying that He lacks power or ability in an absolute sense, but that He chooses to operate only within the parameters of the Father's will.

This shows His voluntary submission to the Father's authority. It's important to note that Jesus is speaking in terms of His earthly ministry, where His works are done in unity with the Father. This speaks to the doctrine of kenosis, as described in Philippians 2:7, where Christ "emptied himself" by taking on human form, becoming obedient to the Father's will.

The statement also reflects the eternal relationship between the Son and the Father within the Trinity. Jesus, though fully divine, operates in perfect harmony with the Father, never acting independently or outside the divine will.

"As I Hear, I Judge"

The next part of the verse, "as I hear, I judge" (kathos akouo krino – Strong's G191, G2919), emphasizes the basis of Jesus' judgment. The verb akouo (Strong's G191) means "to hear," implying that Jesus' judgment comes from His perfect communion with the Father. Jesus listens to the Father and acts accordingly, reflecting their unity in purpose and will.

The verb krino (Strong's G2919), meaning "to judge" or "to make a decision," refers to Jesus' authority to pass judgment, as mentioned earlier in John 5:22: "For the Father judges no one, but has given all judgment to the Son." This judgment is not arbitrary or independent; it is grounded in divine truth, coming directly from the Father.

## "My Judgment is Just"

Jesus goes on to say, "and my judgment is just" (kai he krisis he eme dikaia estin – Strong's G1342), indicating that His judgment is always righteous and fair. The Greek word dikaia (Strong's G1342) means "righteous" or "just," highlighting the perfection of Jesus' decisions because they align with the will of the Father. Jesus is not influenced by selfish motives or human weaknesses. His judgments reflect the very righteousness of God.

In John 7:24, Jesus also emphasizes this point by saying, "Judge not according to appearance, but judge righteous judgment." Here, He invites His followers to emulate this same kind of righteous discernment that is aligned with God's truth, rather than superficial appearances.

"Because I Seek Not Mine Own Will"

The key to understanding why Jesus' judgment is just comes in the latter part of the verse: "because I seek not mine own will, but the will of the Father which hath sent me." The phrase "I seek not mine own will" (ou zeto to thelema to emon – Strong's G2212, G2307) reveals the heart of Christ's mission. The verb zeto (Strong's G2212) means "to seek" or "to strive after." Jesus' primary aim is not to assert His own agenda but to accomplish the will (thelema – Strong's G2307) of the Father.

This complete alignment of wills between Jesus and the Father is a central theme in the Gospels. In John 6:38, Jesus says, "For I came down from heaven, not to do mine own will, but the will of him that sent me." This teaches us that Jesus' life and ministry were driven entirely by His obedience to the Father.

Strong's Concordance Analysis

Breaking down some key Greek terms in John 5:30:

- Do (poiein – Strong's G4160): This verb means "to do" or "to make." In this context, it refers to Jesus' actions, which are entirely in accordance with the Father's will.

- Judge (krino – Strong's G2919): The verb refers to the act of judgment or decision-making. Jesus is appointed by the Father as the Judge of all, as seen in John 5:22.

- Just (dikaia – Strong's G1342): This word is used to describe righteousness or fairness, affirming that Jesus' judgments are in perfect accord with divine justice.

- Will (thelema – Strong's G2307): Refers to a desire or purpose. Jesus submits to the divine will of the Father, not asserting His own separate will but embracing the Father's purpose for His life.

Theological Implications of John 5:30

1. The Unity of the Father and the Son: Jesus' statement in John 5:30 highlights the perfect unity between the Father and the Son. This mutual cooperation is foundational to Trinitarian theology, where the Father, Son, and Holy Spirit share one divine essence while remaining distinct persons.

2. Christ's Obedience to the Father: Jesus models perfect obedience to the Father's will, showing His humility and submission. This obedience is later exemplified in the Garden of Gethsemane, where Jesus prays, "Not my will, but yours be done" (Luke 22:42).

3. The Authority of Christ: Although Jesus declares that He can do nothing on His own, this does not mean He is powerless. Rather, it points to His voluntary submission and alignment with the Father's will. All of Jesus' authority comes from the Father, and His judgments are just because they reflect the Father's truth and righteousness.

4. Judgment and the Role of the Son: Jesus' role as Judge is not independent of the Father. He exercises judgment based on what He hears from the Father, making His judgments perfectly aligned with divine righteousness. This is crucial for understanding the final judgment described in John 5:27: "And he has given him authority to execute judgment, because he is the Son of Man."

Additional Bible Verses on Jesus' Dependence on the Father

- John 14:10: "The words that I say to you I do not speak on my own authority, but the Father who dwells in me does his works." This verse reinforces Jesus' total dependence on the Father for both His words and works.

- John 8:28: "I do nothing on my own authority, but speak just as the Father taught me." Again, Jesus emphasizes that His actions and teachings are not independent but are directly from the Father.

- Hebrews 5:8: "Although he was a son, he learned obedience through what he suffered." This verse illustrates the human aspect of Jesus' obedience, even in suffering.

Practical Application: Walking in the Will of God

The example set by Jesus in John 5:30 calls believers to align their will with God's will. Just as Jesus sought not His own will but the Father's, Christians are called to submit to God's will in their lives. This means seeking God's guidance in decision-making, trusting in His righteousness, and relying on His strength rather than our own.

As we follow Christ's example, we are reminded that true power comes not from asserting our own independence but from submitting to the Father's will. As Jesus declares in

Matthew 26:39, "My Father, if it be possible, let this cup pass from me; nevertheless, not as I will, but as you will."

The Harmony of the Divine Will

John 5:30 offers profound insight into the relationship between Jesus and the Father. Jesus' dependence on the Father is not a sign of weakness but a demonstration of divine unity. All that Jesus does—His works, judgments, and words—flows from the Father's will. This passage invites believers to contemplate the nature of obedience, submission, and the perfect harmony within the Godhead, while also calling us to reflect that same alignment with God's will in our own lives.

CHAPTER 03

---

## JESUS' AUTHORITY TO FORGIVE SINS

*Jesus' Authority to Forgive Sins – An Expository Study of Luke 5:20-21*

Luke 5:20-21 states, "When Jesus saw their faith, He said, 'Man, your sins are forgiven you.' And the scribes and the Pharisees began to question, saying, 'Who is this who speaks blasphemies? Who can forgive sins but God alone?'" This passage highlights a pivotal moment in Jesus' ministry: His proclamation of forgiveness to a paralyzed man and the subsequent reaction of the religious leaders. Their question underscores a central theme of the Gospels—Jesus' divine authority and His unique role as the mediator of God's forgiveness.

Context of Luke 5:20-21

The story in Luke 5:17-26 describes how Jesus was teaching in a crowded house when a group of men, unable to reach Him due to the large crowd, lowered a paralyzed man through the roof so that he might be healed. Moved by their faith, Jesus responds by forgiving the man's sins before healing him physically. This act of forgiving sins shocks the Pharisees and teachers of the law, who view such an action as blasphemous, since only God has the authority to forgive sins.

"When Jesus Saw Their Faith"

In Luke 5:20, it says, "When Jesus saw their faith, He said, 'Man, your sins are forgiven you.'" The phrase "saw their faith" (idōn tēn pistin autōn – Strong's G1492, G4102) indicates that Jesus recognized the collective faith of the men who brought the paralyzed man. The Greek verb idōn (Strong's G1492) means "to see" or "to perceive," which shows that Jesus discerned not only their physical actions but also the deeper spiritual trust they had in Him.

Faith (pistis – Strong's G4102), in this context, goes beyond mere belief. It involves an active trust that Jesus could heal and help, demonstrating a confidence in His divine power. This aligns with other passages in the Gospels, where faith is often the precondition for receiving healing or other blessings from Jesus. For instance, in Matthew 9:29, Jesus tells two blind men, "According to your faith be it unto you."

"Your Sins Are Forgiven You"

Jesus' declaration, "Your sins are forgiven you" (aphēntai soi hai hamartiai sou – Strong's G863, G4675), is a startling one. The Greek word for "forgiven" is aphēntai (Strong's G863), which means "to send away," "to dismiss," or "to release." In a theological sense, it refers to the cancellation of sin's guilt and penalty.

Sin (hamartia – Strong's G266) refers to any action, attitude, or thought that falls short of God's moral standard. In this instance, Jesus addresses the man's spiritual condition first, implying that his paralysis is not merely a physical affliction but also has a deeper connection to his sinful state. By forgiving his sins, Jesus is addressing the root of human suffering—sin itself.

The Reaction of the Pharisees: "Who Can Forgive Sins But God Alone?"

The response of the scribes and Pharisees in Luke 5:21 is telling. They say, "Who is this who speaks blasphemies? Who can forgive sins but God alone?" The charge of blasphemy (blasphēmia – Strong's G988) is serious because, in Jewish law, it is an offense punishable by death (Leviticus 24:16). To claim the power to forgive sins was, in their view, to claim an authority reserved for God Himself.

Their question—"Who can forgive sins but God alone?"—is both a theological truth and a challenge. Theologically, they are correct. Forgiveness of sins is an exclusive prerogative of God, as seen in verses like Isaiah 43:25, where God says, "I, even I, am He who blots out your transgressions, for my own sake, and remembers your sins no more." This statement underscores that forgiveness is an act of divine grace.

However, the Pharisees failed to recognize that Jesus, by virtue of His divine nature, had the authority to forgive sins. Jesus' actions here reveal His identity as both the Son of God and the Messiah. In forgiving the man's sins, Jesus is making a profound theological claim: He is God incarnate, with all the authority that belongs to God.

## Jesus' Authority to Forgive Sins

The key to understanding this passage is the recognition of Jesus' authority. The authority to forgive sins is not something that Jesus claims in isolation. Rather, it is tied to His identity as the Son of God and His role as the Savior of humanity. In Mark 2:10, a parallel account of this event, Jesus explicitly states, "But that you may know that the Son of Man has authority on earth to forgive sins..." The term "Son of Man" refers to Jesus' Messianic identity (see Daniel

7:13-14) and His role as the one appointed by God to bring salvation to the world.

Jesus' authority to forgive sins is further confirmed in His resurrection, which vindicates His claims. As Paul writes in Romans 4:25, "He was delivered over to death for our sins and was raised to life for our justification." The resurrection serves as proof that Jesus' work of atonement was effective, and that He has the power to forgive and justify sinners.

Strong's Concordance Analysis

Here is a closer look at some key Greek terms used in this passage:

- Faith (pistis – Strong's G4102): Faith in the New Testament is often a condition for receiving healing or forgiveness. In this passage, the faith of the men who brought the paralytic demonstrates their confidence in Jesus' power.

- Forgive (aphēntai – Strong's G863): This term means "to send away" or "to release," and it is used in the New Testament to describe the act of forgiving sins.

- Sin (hamartia – Strong's G266): The Greek word for sin refers to missing the mark of God's standard. In this context, Jesus addresses the man's sin before dealing with his physical condition.

- Blasphemy (blasphēmia — Strong's G988): Blasphemy refers to speaking irreverently about God. The Pharisees accuse Jesus of blasphemy because they believe only God has the right to forgive sins.

Jesus' Divinity and the Forgiveness of Sins

The question posed by the Pharisees—"Who can forgive sins but God alone?"—is crucial for understanding the nature of Jesus' mission. By forgiving sins, Jesus is not only healing physical ailments but addressing the deeper issue of humanity's estrangement from God. Sin is ultimately an offense against God (Psalm 51:4), and only God can truly absolve a person from guilt.

By declaring that the man's sins are forgiven, Jesus is demonstrating that He possesses the authority of God Himself. This is a direct claim to His divinity, which the Pharisees understood but refused to accept. Throughout the Gospels, Jesus' authority to forgive sins is a central element of His Messianic identity.

In John 1:29, John the Baptist declares, "Behold, the Lamb of God, who takes away the sin of the world!" This statement echoes Jesus' role as the one who can remove sin, a role that belongs solely to God. By forgiving sins during His earthly ministry, Jesus is providing a foretaste of the greater atonement He would accomplish through His death on the cross. This atonement is what makes the forgiveness of sins possible for all who believe in Him.

The Connection Between Forgiveness and Healing

A key aspect of this story in Luke 5 is the connection between the forgiveness of sins and physical healing. When Jesus forgives the man's sins, He is addressing the spiritual cause of his suffering. In Jewish thought, sickness and suffering were often viewed as consequences of sin (see John 9:2, where the disciples ask Jesus about a blind man, "Who sinned, this man or his parents, that he was born blind?"). Although Jesus does not affirm this worldview in every case (as in John 9:3, where He rejects the idea that sin caused the man's blindness), in this instance, He treats the man's spiritual condition as the first issue to be resolved.

After forgiving the man's sins, Jesus goes on to heal him physically, commanding him to "rise, pick up your bed and go home" (Luke 5:24). The immediate physical healing is a sign that Jesus has the authority not only to heal the body but to forgive sin, which is the deeper need. This miraculous healing serves as confirmation of His divine authority, as seen in the following verse: "And immediately he rose up before them and picked up what he had been lying on and went home, glorifying God" (Luke 5:25).

Jesus' ability to heal demonstrates His mastery over both the physical and spiritual realms. This dual authority points to His identity as the incarnate Son of God, who has come to restore the whole person—body and soul.

The Pharisees' Error: Rejecting Jesus' Authority

The Pharisees' reaction to Jesus' proclamation of forgiveness exposes their inability to recognize Him as the Messiah. Their question—"Who can forgive sins but God alone?"—reveals both their understanding of God's sovereignty and their failure to grasp the significance of Jesus' actions. While they are correct that only God can forgive sins, they fail to see that Jesus, as the Son of God, possesses this divine authority.

This rejection of Jesus' authority is a recurring theme in the Gospels. The religious leaders often challenge Jesus, questioning His authority to perform miracles, teach with authority, and forgive sins. Their refusal to accept Jesus as the Messiah leads to their eventual role in His crucifixion, but even this fulfills the divine plan of salvation.

In contrast to the Pharisees, the people who witnessed the miracle glorified God, recognizing the power and authority at work in Jesus. Luke 5:26 states, "Amazement seized them all, and they glorified God and were filled with awe, saying, 'We have seen extraordinary things today.'" Their reaction stands in stark contrast to the skeptical and hostile response of the religious leaders. The crowd saw in Jesus the revelation of God's power, while the Pharisees only saw a threat to their authority.

# Jesus as the Ultimate Mediator of Forgiveness

The broader theological significance of this passage lies in Jesus' role as the mediator between God and humanity. In the Old Testament, the priesthood played a central role in mediating between God and the people, especially through the sacrificial system. The high priest would offer sacrifices for the atonement of sins, but this system was temporary and pointed forward to a greater fulfillment.

In Hebrews 10:11-12, we read: "And every priest stands daily at his service, offering repeatedly the same sacrifices, which can never take away sins. But when Christ had offered for all time a single sacrifice for sins, He sat down at the right hand of God." Jesus, through His death and resurrection, fulfills and supersedes the Old Testament sacrificial system. His sacrifice is the final and complete atonement for sin, making Him the ultimate mediator of forgiveness.

In 1 Timothy 2:5, Paul writes, "For there is one God, and there is one mediator between God and men, the man Christ Jesus." This emphasizes Jesus' unique role as the one who reconciles humanity to God. His authority to forgive sins is a direct result of His work as the mediator of the New Covenant, established through His blood (see Hebrews 9:15).

Implications for Believers Today

The forgiveness of sins is at the heart of the Christian gospel. Jesus' declaration to the paralyzed man in Luke 5:20—"Your sins are forgiven you"—is a message that echoes through the ages. Just as Jesus forgave the man's sins, He offers forgiveness to all who come to Him in faith. This forgiveness is not earned by good works or religious observance but is a gift of grace, made possible by Jesus' sacrifice on the cross.

For believers, the forgiveness of sins brings reconciliation with God and freedom from guilt and shame. As Paul writes in Ephesians 1:7, "In Him we have redemption through His blood, the forgiveness of our trespasses, according to the riches of His grace." This forgiveness restores our relationship with God and enables us to live in the fullness of His grace.

Furthermore, Jesus' authority to forgive sins serves as a reminder of His divinity and His role as Lord over all creation. As believers, we are called to acknowledge Jesus not only as Savior but also as Lord, submitting to His authority in every area of our lives. His authority over sin and death assures us that He has the power to deliver us from the bondage of sin and to bring us into eternal life.

The Authority of Jesus to Forgive Sins

The account of Jesus forgiving the paralyzed man's sins in Luke 5:20-21 is a powerful demonstration of His divine authority. By proclaiming forgiveness, Jesus asserts His identity as the Son of God and the Savior of the world. The reaction of the Pharisees—"Who can forgive sins but God alone?"—highlights the central truth of the gospel: Jesus is God in the flesh, with the power to forgive sins and restore humanity to right relationship with God.

This passage invites us to reflect on the depth of Jesus' love and the magnitude of His sacrifice. His authority to forgive sins is not only a testimony to His divinity but also a profound gift to all who put their faith in Him. Just as the paralyzed man received both spiritual and physical healing, we too can experience the transformative power of Jesus' forgiveness in our lives. Through faith in Christ, we are reconciled to God, freed from sin, and empowered to live in His grace.

As we consider the question posed by the Pharisees—"Who can forgive sins but God alone?"—we are reminded of the truth proclaimed throughout the New Testament: Jesus is both fully God and fully man, the one who has come to take away the sins of the world. "In Him we have redemption through His blood, the forgiveness of sins, according to the riches of His grace" (Ephesians 1:7).

CHAPTER 04

---

# JESUS' EQUALITY WITH GOD BEFORE HIS INCARNATION

*Expository Study and Comprehensive Commentary on Philippians 2:5-8*

The passage in Philippians 2:5-8 presents one of the most profound theological truths of the New Testament: the pre-existence of Christ in the form of God, His voluntary humility in becoming human, and His ultimate exaltation by God. This passage is often referred to as the "Christ Hymn" and offers a rich insight into the mystery of the Incarnation—how the eternal Son of God, equal with God in His divine nature, took on human flesh.

Text of Philippians 2:5-8 (ESV):

"Have this mind among yourselves, which is yours in Christ Jesus, who, though he was in the form of God, did not count equality with God a thing to be grasped,

but emptied himself, by taking the form of a servant, being born in the likeness of men.

And being found in human form, he humbled himself by becoming obedient to the point of death, even death on a cross."

*Verse 5: "Have this mind among yourselves, which is yours in Christ Jesus."*

Paul begins this section by calling believers to adopt the mindset or attitude that was in Christ Jesus. The word for "mind" here is φρονέω (Strong's G5426), meaning to think, regard, or have a particular perspective. Paul is urging the Philippians to adopt Christ's humility and selflessness. The attitude of Christ is characterized by His willingness to set aside His rights and privileges as God for the sake of others, an example for all believers to follow.

This sets the stage for the unfolding description of Christ's condescension from divine glory to human form.

*Verse 6: "Who, though he was in the form of God, did not count equality with God a thing to be grasped."*

The phrase "in the form of God" (Greek: μορφή θεοῦ; Strong's G3444 for μορφή and G2316 for θεός) reveals that Jesus existed in the essential nature of God. The word μορφή refers to the outward expression of an inward reality. It indicates that Christ had the very nature and attributes of God. This aligns with passages such as John 1:1, which declares, "In the beginning was the Word, and the Word was with God, and the Word was God."

The second part of this verse, "did not count equality with God a thing to be grasped," shows that although Jesus was equal with God, He did not consider this equality something to be used for His own advantage or selfishly held onto. The word "grasped" is translated from the Greek term ἁρπαγμός (Strong's G725), which can mean to seize or hold tightly. Jesus, although fully divine, did not cling to His rights as God; rather, He was willing to set them aside in His incarnation.

This reflects a profound humility and love. Christ, being equal with God, had every right to remain in the exalted state of divine glory. Yet He chose not to assert His rights but instead surrendered them for the sake of human redemption. This contrasts sharply with humanity's natural tendency to cling to status and power.

*Verse 7: "But emptied himself, by taking the form of a servant, being born in the likeness of men."*

The phrase "emptied himself" comes from the Greek verb κενόω (Strong's G2758), meaning to make empty or to divest oneself of privileges. This is often referred to as the kenosis, a theological term derived from this verse. Christ's "emptying" does not mean that He ceased to be God or relinquished His divine attributes, but that He laid aside His divine privileges and prerogatives. He veiled His divine glory and took on the limitations of humanity.

This is emphasized by the phrase "taking the form of a servant" (Greek: μορφὴν δούλου; Strong's G3444 for μορφή and G1401 for δοῦλος). The same word μορφή (form) is used here as in verse 6, indicating that just as Jesus was in the form of God, He also fully took on the nature of a servant. This was not merely a change in appearance but a genuine assumption of the human condition, including the role of servanthood. Jesus didn't come as a ruler or king but as a servant, fulfilling prophecies like Isaiah 53:11, which describes the Messiah as the "Suffering Servant."

"Being born in the likeness of men" (Greek: ὁμοίωμα; Strong's G3667) refers to Jesus' incarnation, emphasizing that He was truly human. He did not simply appear as a man; He was born fully human while remaining fully divine. This mystery is encapsulated in the doctrine of the hypostatic union, which teaches that Jesus is one person with two natures—divine and human.

*Verse 8: "And being found in human form, he humbled himself by becoming obedient to the point of death, even death on a cross."*

This verse continues the theme of Christ's humility. The phrase "being found in human form" (Greek: σχήματι; Strong's G4976) refers to His outward appearance as a man. Even though Jesus was fully God, His divine glory was not obvious during His earthly ministry; instead, He was perceived by others as an ordinary human being.

"He humbled himself"—the Greek word here for humble is ταπεινόω (Strong's G5013), which means to lower oneself, to submit willingly to a lower state. Christ's humility is demonstrated not only in becoming a man but also in His willingness to submit to the most humiliating and painful death imaginable—crucifixion. Crucifixion was reserved for the lowest of criminals and was considered the most degrading form of punishment in the Roman world.

The phrase "obedient to the point of death" highlights Jesus' submission to the Father's will. As seen in Hebrews 5:8, "Although He was a Son, He learned obedience through what He suffered." Jesus' obedience was not merely passive; it was an active submission to the divine plan of salvation. This obedience took Him all the way to the cross, where He bore the sins of humanity (see 1 Peter 2:24).

"Even death on a cross" emphasizes the extremity of Christ's humility and sacrifice. Crucifixion was the most shameful and excruciating form of execution, yet Jesus endured it willingly for the sake of humanity's redemption. As Paul writes in Galatians 3:13, "Christ redeemed us from the curse of the law by becoming a curse for us." His death on the cross was not only a physical suffering but also a spiritual one, as He took upon Himself the sins of the world (see 2 Corinthians 5:21).

# Theological Implications of Philippians 2:5-8

1. The Pre-existence and Divinity of Christ

This passage clearly teaches that Christ existed in the "form of God" before His incarnation. This affirms His pre-existence and His equality with God the Father. Verses like John 17:5, where Jesus prays, "Father, glorify me in your own presence with the glory that I had with you before the world existed," reinforce the eternal divinity of Christ. He did not begin to exist at His birth in Bethlehem but existed from all eternity as the second Person of the Trinity.

2. The Humility of Christ

The kenosis of Christ—His self-emptying—reveals the depth of His humility. Although He had every right to maintain His divine status, He chose to become a servant and suffer for the sake of others. This sets the supreme example of humility for all believers. As Matthew 20:28 states, "The Son of Man came not to be served but to serve, and to give His life as a ransom for many."

### 3. Christ's Humanity

Jesus fully assumed human nature, including its weaknesses and limitations (though without sin). His identification with humanity is seen in passages like Hebrews 4:15, which declares, "For we do not have a high priest who is unable to sympathize with our weaknesses, but one who in every respect has been tempted as we are, yet without sin." His full humanity is essential for His role as the mediator between God and man (see 1 Timothy 2:5).

### 4. Christ's Obedience and Sacrifice

Jesus' obedience to the Father, even to the point of death on the cross, is central to the doctrine of salvation. His death was not merely a martyrdom but an atoning sacrifice for the sins of the world. As Isaiah 53:5 prophesied, "He was pierced for our transgressions; He was crushed for our iniquities; upon Him was the chastisement that brought us peace, and with His wounds, we are healed."

# The Majesty of Christ's Humility and Exaltation

Philippians 2:5-8 provides a powerful and rich Christological framework that reveals both the divine nature of Jesus and the depth of His humility. Several key theological implications arise from this passage:

1. The Pre-existence and Divinity of Christ

Christ's equality with God before His incarnation is undeniable from this text. The phrase "in the form of God" (μορφὴ θεοῦ) points to His essential nature as divine. Jesus is not merely a representative of God but shares in the very nature and glory of God Himself, as affirmed in John 1:1 ("the Word was God") and Colossians 1:15 (Christ is "the image of the invisible God"). The fact that He did not consider equality with God something to be "grasped" or clung to speaks to His unique position as divine.

2. Kenosis: The Self-Emptying of Christ

The kenosis or self-emptying of Christ is one of the greatest mysteries of the Christian faith. In Philippians 2:7, Paul uses the term κενόω to describe how Christ willingly set aside His divine privileges without ceasing to be God. This does not mean that Christ surrendered His divinity but that He took on the limitations of humanity. He veiled His divine glory and became fully human while remaining fully divine, in a manner that still preserved His equality with God the Father. This truth is echoed in the incarnation described in John 1:14: "The Word became flesh and dwelt among us."

3. The Incarnation and Servanthood of Christ

In becoming human, Christ "took the form of a servant" (μορφὴν δούλου). This servant-role emphasizes His willingness to submit Himself to the will of the Father, as He embodied the Suffering Servant prophesied in Isaiah 53. Jesus came not to be served but to serve, and His entire earthly life exemplified sacrificial service to others, culminating in His death on the cross (see Matthew 20:28). He was not born into wealth or power but into humble circumstances, demonstrating that His kingdom operates by a different set of values than the world's.

4. Christ's Obedience and Sacrifice

Christ's obedience to the Father is a central theme in this passage. His humility and obedience led Him to "the point of death, even death on a cross" (Philippians 2:8). The cross represents the ultimate act of humiliation and suffering, and yet it was through this act that the salvation of humanity was accomplished. The depth of Christ's love is seen in His willingness to endure such shame and agony for the sake of reconciling sinners to God. His obedience fulfills the Father's redemptive plan, as foretold in Isaiah 53:10: "It was the will of the LORD to crush him; he has put him to grief."

5. The Example for Believers

Paul's primary exhortation in this passage is for believers to adopt the mindset of Christ. Just as Christ did not cling to His rights and privileges, believers are called to live lives of humility, selflessness, and service to others. Jesus' self-emptying and His servanthood are the model for Christian conduct. As Paul says in Philippians 2:3-4, we are to "do nothing from selfish ambition or conceit, but in humility count others more significant than yourselves. Let each of you look not only to his own interests, but also to the interests of others." The Christian life is one of humble service, following the example set by our Lord.

6. The Exaltation of Christ (Philippians 2:9-11)

Although this study focuses primarily on Philippians 2:5-8, the passage must be understood in the broader context of the subsequent verses, which describe Christ's exaltation. Philippians 2:9-11 reveals that because of Christ's humility and obedience, God has "highly exalted him and bestowed on him the name that is above every name" (verse 9). This exaltation includes Christ's resurrection, ascension, and His current reign at the right hand of God (see Hebrews 1:3). Ultimately, every knee will bow, and every tongue will confess that "Jesus Christ is Lord, to the glory of God the Father" (verse 11). The pathway of humility led to the greatest exaltation, and this pattern is also promised to those who humble themselves before God (see James 4:10).

Final Reflection:

The truths found in Philippians 2:5-8 challenge believers to contemplate the infinite majesty of Christ's divinity and His humility in becoming man. Though He existed in the form of God, Jesus did not cling to His status but humbled Himself, taking on the likeness of human flesh to serve, suffer, and ultimately save. His life stands as the ultimate example of sacrificial love and humility, calling all believers to follow in His footsteps.

The mystery of the Incarnation reveals the heart of God: a heart willing to endure the humiliation of the cross for the sake of redeeming humanity. In following Christ's example, we are called to empty ourselves of pride and ambition, serve others, and live lives of humble obedience to the will of God.

The kenosis of Christ, His self-emptying for the sake of love, and His exaltation by the Father form the core of the Christian understanding of the Gospel. This passage reminds us that the road to glory is paved with humility, service, and obedience to God's will.

**Key Cross-References:**

- John 1:1, 14 – The pre-existent Word was with God and became flesh.

- Colossians 1:15-20 – Christ is the image of the invisible God, pre-eminent over creation.

- Isaiah 53:3-12 – The Suffering Servant who bore the sins of many.

- Matthew 20:28 – The Son of Man came to serve and give His life as a ransom.

- Hebrews 1:3 – Jesus upholds the universe by His word and is seated at the right hand of God.

- 2 Corinthians 8:9 – Jesus became poor for our sake, though He was rich in glory.

- Galatians 3:13 – Christ became a curse for us by dying on the cross.

- 1 Peter 2:21-24 – Jesus' example of suffering and obedience, bearing our sins on the cross.

In conclusion, Philippians 2:5-8 offers a majestic glimpse into the mystery of the Incarnation, providing believers with a model for Christ-like humility and service. As we reflect on Christ's example, we are reminded of the immense love and sacrifice involved in His becoming human and the eternal glory that awaited Him after His obedience to death. Through this, we are called to embody the same humility and love, trusting that God exalts those who humble themselves before Him.

# CHAPTER 05

## JESUS' CLAIM TO DIVINITY AS THE SON OF GOD (JOHN 5:18)

In John 5:18, the Jews' reaction to Jesus' claim to be the Son of God reveals their understanding that He was making Himself equal with God. This passage plays a crucial role in affirming the divinity of Christ and the unique relationship between the Father and the Son. Through an expository study, comprehensive commentary, and the use of the Strong's Concordance, we will explore the theological and doctrinal significance of Jesus' claim to be the Son of God.

I. Context of the Passage (John 5:1-17)

The broader context of John 5 provides the background for the conflict between Jesus and the Jewish leaders. The chapter begins with Jesus healing a man at the Pool of Bethesda, a miracle that ignited controversy because it occurred on the Sabbath (John 5:1-9). When the Jewish authorities confronted the healed man, he pointed to Jesus as the one who had healed him. Upon finding out that it was Jesus, the Jews sought to persecute Him for violating the Sabbath law (John 5:16).

In response to their accusations, Jesus made a profound statement: "My Father is working until now, and I am working" (John 5:17, ESV). By calling God "My Father," Jesus was making a claim that went beyond mere servanthood or prophetic office. He was asserting a unique, intimate relationship with God that implied equality with Him.

II. Jesus' Claim of Equality with God (John 5:18)

John 5:18 states: "This was why the Jews were seeking all the more to kill him, because not only was he breaking the Sabbath, but he was even calling God his own Father, making himself equal with God" (ESV). Here, we see that the Jewish leaders understood Jesus' claim clearly and reacted strongly because it suggested that Jesus was not merely a man, prophet, or healer but was asserting divine status.

- "Calling God His own Father" (Greek: πατέρα ἴδιον – patera idion). The word ἴδιον (idion, G2398) means "one's own" or "peculiar to oneself." Jesus was not speaking in a general sense of God as Father (as in "our Father") but rather emphasizing a special and unique relationship. This use of ἴδιον conveyed to the Jews that Jesus was asserting a divine sonship that was exclusive and intimate.

- "Making Himself equal with God" (Greek: ἴσον ἑαυτὸν ποιῶν τῷ θεῷ – ison heauton poion tō theō). The word ἴσον (ison, G2470) means "equal" or "on par." The Jews understood that Jesus' claim of divine sonship meant that He was asserting equality with God in essence, authority, and nature. This was a direct challenge to their monotheistic understanding of God, hence their outrage.

III. Theological Implications of Jesus' Claim

The implications of Jesus claiming to be the Son of God and equal with the Father are profound and foundational to Christian theology.

1. Jesus as the Divine Son of God

- The title "Son of God" (Greek: υἱὸς τοῦ θεοῦ – huios tou theou) is not merely metaphorical but signifies the unique relationship between Jesus and the Father. In this claim, Jesus is declaring His participation in the divine nature. In John 10:30, He says, "I and the Father are one," underscoring His divine unity with God.

- The Jews, with their understanding of monotheism, could not accept the idea of God having a divine Son without it implying polytheism. However, Jesus' claim does not suggest two separate gods but rather a complex unity within the Godhead, as later formulated in the doctrine of the Trinity.

2. Jesus' Authority to Act as God

- In John 5:19-23, Jesus further elaborates on His equality with the Father. He declares that He does nothing of His own accord but only what He sees the Father doing. This establishes the perfect harmony and unity of action between the Father and the Son.

- In John 5:22, Jesus asserts that the Father "has given all judgment to the Son" (ESV). The ability to judge the world is a prerogative of God alone, and by declaring that judgment is entrusted to Him, Jesus is asserting His divine authority.

- The Strong's Concordance gives insight into the word "judgment" (Greek: κρίσιν – krisin, G2920), which refers to the process of deciding, especially in a divine or final sense. By claiming this role, Jesus is taking on a function that belongs solely to God.

3. The Doctrine of the Trinity

- The relationship between Jesus and the Father as described in John 5:18-23 serves as a critical foundation for the doctrine of the Trinity. Jesus is distinct from the Father in

His personhood, yet He shares the same divine essence. This mutual indwelling and shared authority point to the Trinitarian understanding of one God in three persons (Father, Son, and Holy Spirit).

- Other passages such as John 1:1-2, John 8:58, and Colossians 1:15-20 further affirm the eternal pre-existence and divinity of Christ, supporting His claim in John 5:18 to be equal with God.

IV. Scriptural Cross-References to Jesus' Divinity

To further illustrate the divinity of Christ and His claim to be the Son of God, we can turn to several key scriptures:

1. John 1:1-14 – The prologue of John's Gospel states that "the Word was with God, and the Word was God" (John 1:1). This identifies Jesus (the Word) as co-eternal and co-equal with God. In verse 14, the Word becomes flesh, confirming that Jesus is the incarnation of the divine Logos.

2. John 10:30-33 – Jesus explicitly says, "I and the Father are one," leading the Jews to accuse Him of blasphemy, saying, "You, being a man, make yourself God" (John 10:33). This passage further cements the Jews' understanding that Jesus claimed divine status.

3. John 8:58 – Jesus declares, "Before Abraham was, I am." The use of "I am" (Greek: ἐγώ εἰμι – egō eimi, G1510)

refers back to the divine name revealed to Moses in Exodus 3:14 (YHWH, the "I Am"). By using this term, Jesus was making an explicit claim to eternal existence and divinity.

4. Colossians 2:9 – Paul writes that in Christ "the whole fullness of deity dwells bodily." This affirms that Jesus possesses the full nature of God, not merely part of it or a reflection of it.

V. Jewish Reaction and Opposition

The reaction of the Jewish leaders in John 5:18 is indicative of their refusal to accept Jesus' claims to divinity. Their desire to kill Him stems not only from His perceived violation of the Sabbath but from what they saw as blasphemy. According to the Law of Moses, blasphemy—claiming equality with God—was punishable by death (see Leviticus 24:16).

This opposition to Jesus' divine claims continues throughout His ministry, culminating in His trial before the Sanhedrin, where the high priest asked, "Are you the Christ, the Son of the Blessed?" (Mark 14:61, ESV). Jesus' affirmative response ("I am") was met with charges of blasphemy and ultimately led to His crucifixion (Mark 14:62-64).

*Jesus as the Divine Son of God*

In John 5:18, Jesus' claim to be the Son of God is inseparable from His claim to divinity. By calling God "His own Father," Jesus was asserting a unique and intimate relationship that implied equality with God. The Jewish leaders correctly understood this as a claim to be divine, which led to their desire to kill Him. This passage is crucial in understanding the Christian doctrine of Christ's divinity and His equality with the Father.

Through the lens of the Strong's Concordance and cross-references, we can see how this claim is affirmed throughout the New Testament. Jesus, the eternal Son of God, shares in the fullness of the divine nature, exercises divine authority, and calls His followers to recognize His unique status as God incarnate. His claim in John 5:18 points directly to the foundational Christian belief in the Trinity and the co-equality of the Father, Son, and Holy Spirit.

CHAPTER 06

---

# JESUS AS THE "I AM"

*Jesus as the "I AM" – The Divine, Eternal Existence of Christ*

The phrase "I AM" carries profound theological implications about God's eternal self-existence, a truth first revealed in Exodus 3:14-15 when God identified Himself as "I AM THAT I AM" (Hebrew: אֶהְיֶה אֲשֶׁר אֶהְיֶה – Ehyeh Asher Ehyeh). This divine name, YHWH (Yahweh or Jehovah), is intrinsically tied to God's eternal and independent nature. In the New Testament, Jesus used the same designation "I AM" in John 8:24 and John 8:58, which prompted the Jews to accuse Him of blasphemy, for they understood this as a claim to divinity. Jesus' use of "I AM" directly connects Him to YHWH, confirming His divine nature and eternal existence.

This chapter will examine John 8:24, 58, and Exodus 3:14-15, providing an expository study, commentary, and analysis using the Strong's Concordance to delve into the depth of Jesus' claim to divinity and His eternal existence.

I. The Divine Name in Exodus 3:14-15

In Exodus 3:14, when Moses asked for God's name, God responded: "I AM THAT I AM" (Hebrew: אֶהְיֶה אֲשֶׁר אֶהְיֶה, Ehyeh Asher Ehyeh), which translates to "I will be what I will be" or simply "I AM". This name points to God's self-existence, unchanging nature, and eternal being.

- Strong's Concordance on "I AM" (Hebrew: אֶהְיֶה, Ehyeh, H1961) derives from the verb הָיָה (hayah), meaning "to be" or "to exist." It signifies that God exists independently of all creation and is not bound by time or space.

- YHWH (Hebrew: יהוה, Yahweh or Jehovah, H3068) is the personal name of God. It comes from the same root as Ehyeh and conveys God's eternal, self-sufficient existence. The name YHWH is often rendered as "LORD" in most English translations.

Exodus 3:15 says: "The LORD [YHWH]…this is my name forever" (KJV). God reveals His name as YHWH, affirming His eternal nature. Throughout the Old Testament, YHWH is depicted as the Creator, Sustainer, and the only true God.

II. Jesus as the "I AM" in John 8:24 and John 8:58

In John 8, Jesus confronts the religious leaders of His day, and He makes two significant statements using the divine name "I AM", thus claiming equality with YHWH.

1. John 8:24: "Therefore I said to you that you will die in your sins; for unless you believe that I am He, you will die in your sins" (NASB).

- The phrase "I am He" (Greek: ἐγώ εἰμι, egō eimi, G1473 + G1510) translates directly as "I AM" in Greek. Jesus is making an absolute claim to be the eternal God. The Strong's Concordance notes:

- ἐγώ (egō, G1473) means "I."

- εἰμι (eimi, G1510) means "to be" or "to exist." Combined, "ἐγώ εἰμι" is the Greek equivalent of God's declaration "I AM" in Exodus 3:14.

By using "I AM" in this context, Jesus asserts that belief in His divine nature is essential for salvation. He is declaring that without recognizing Him as the eternal, self-existent One, people will remain in their sins and face eternal separation from God.

2. John 8:58: "Jesus said to them, 'Truly, truly, I say to you, before Abraham was, I am'" (ESV).

- The Jews had questioned Jesus' authority, particularly in relation to Abraham, their patriarch. Jesus responded by using "I AM" once again, this time asserting His pre-existence before Abraham.

- Strong's Concordance shows that the phrase "I am" (Greek: ἐγώ εἰμι, cgō cimi, G1473 + G1510) in this verse reflects the same divine name used in Exodus 3:14. Jesus claims not only pre-existence before Abraham but also an eternal existence that transcends time.

- The Jews understood Jesus' statement as a claim to divinity, which is why they picked up stones to kill Him (John 8:59). According to Levitical law, blasphemy—claiming to be God—was punishable by death (Leviticus 24:16).

III. The Father and the Son as YHWH

The name YHWH (I AM) is shared by both the Father and the Son, affirming their co-equal and co-eternal nature while maintaining their distinct personhood.

1. The Father as YHWH:

- Isaiah 42:8: "I am the LORD; that is my name!" (ESV). The Father identifies Himself by the divine name YHWH, reinforcing His eternal, self-existent nature.

2. The Son as YHWH:

- John 8:58: Jesus, by declaring "I AM", identifies Himself as YHWH, the same God who spoke to Moses in the burning bush.

While the Father and the Son share the same divine name and nature, they are distinct persons within the Godhead. This reflects the doctrine of the Trinity, where the Father, Son, and Holy Spirit are one in essence but distinct in person.

Just as an earthly father and son may share the same name but are distinct individuals, so too are the Father and the Son distinct persons who share the same divine nature. This does not mean they are separate gods but rather two persons within the one God.

IV. Scriptural Cross-References to the Divinity of Jesus

1. Colossians 1:16-17: Paul affirms that Jesus is the Creator of all things, saying, "For by him all things were created... He is before all things, and in him all things hold together" (ESV). This emphasizes Jesus' pre-existence and divine role as Creator, consistent with His claim to be the eternal "I AM."

2. John 1:1-3: "In the beginning was the Word, and the Word was with God, and the Word was God... All things

were made through him" (ESV). Here, Jesus (the Word) is identified as eternal and divine, co-equal with the Father.

3. Hebrews 1:3: The Son is "the radiance of the glory of God and the exact imprint of his nature" (ESV). Jesus perfectly represents God because He shares the same divine essence as YHWH.

V. The Jewish Response to Jesus' Claims

Throughout the Gospel of John, the Jewish leaders' reactions to Jesus' statements highlight their understanding of His claims to divinity. In John 8:59, the Jews attempt to stone Jesus for blasphemy, showing that they fully understood He was claiming to be God. Their response reflects the gravity of the claim, as blasphemy—equating oneself with God—was a capital offense under Jewish law.

Similar reactions occur in John 10:30-33, where Jesus says, "I and the Father are one", and the Jews again pick up stones to kill Him, accusing Him of making Himself God. These hostile reactions demonstrate the Jews' clear understanding that Jesus was claiming to be the divine Son of God, equal with YHWH.

VI. Conclusion: Jesus as the Eternal I AM

In both Exodus 3:14-15 and John 8:24, 58, the name "I AM" reveals the eternal, self-existent nature of God. Jesus' use of the same name in the New Testament affirms His divinity and equality with the Father. The Jewish leaders understood these claims, and their violent reactions show that Jesus was not misunderstood—He was clearly asserting His divine identity as YHWH.

Jesus, the eternal Son of God, shares the divine name and nature of YHWH, making Him fully God, alongside the Father. While distinct in person, the Father and Son are united in essence, both bearing the name "I AM"—the eternal, self-existent One. This truth lies at the heart of the Christian faith: that Jesus is not only the Savior but also the divine, eternal God, the same YHWH who revealed Himself to Moses and who continues to reign as Lord of all.

This chapter has explored the profound significance of Jesus' claim to be the "I AM

Just as the prospectors were beginning to settle into their new way of life, nature unleashed its fury upon the boomtown with a vengeance. A dark and ominous storm cloud, pregnant with rain, loomed on the horizon, and the wind whispered foreboding tales of what was to come.

This expository study of Exodus 3:14-15 and John 8:24, 58 affirms the eternal, self-existent nature of Jesus as the divine "I AM." Understanding Jesus as YHWH is central to Christian theology, for it affirms that He is not merely a prophet or teacher but the eternal God, co-equal with the Father, who existed before time and will continue for eternity. The eternal existence of both the Father and the Son, as YHWH, reveals the mystery of the Godhead—distinct in person, one in essence, and eternal in nature.

CHAPTER 07

## JESUS CHRIST – THE ROCK OF SALVATION

*Jesus Christ – The Rock of Salvation: A Comprehensive Study of YHWH as the Rock in Scripture*

In both the Old and New Testaments, God is repeatedly called "the Rock," symbolizing His strength, stability, and reliability as the protector and savior of His people. The Hebrew Scriptures often describe YHWH (Yahweh) as the Rock who cared for Israel, and in the New Testament, Paul refers to Christ as the Rock who followed and sustained the Israelites. This continuity of the Rock imagery across both testaments highlights the unity of God's nature and the centrality of Christ in the divine plan of salvation.

This chapter will offer an expository study and comprehensive commentary on the references to YHWH as the Rock in the Old Testament and how the Apostle Paul identifies Christ as the Rock in the New Testament. Using Strong's Concordance and other cross-references, we will explore the depth of this metaphor and its theological implications for understanding the nature of God and the divinity of Christ.

I. YHWH as the Rock in the Old Testament

1. Deuteronomy 32:3-4:

- "For I proclaim the name of the LORD: Ascribe greatness to our God. He is the Rock, His work is perfect; For all His ways are justice, A God of truth and without injustice; Righteous and upright is He" (NKJV).

In Moses' song, YHWH is called the "Rock" (Hebrew: צוּר, tsur, H6697), a metaphor used to describe God's unshakable and steadfast nature. God is immovable, dependable, and provides shelter and protection for His people. The Strong's Concordance definition of tsur points to a rock or a cliff, indicating strength and stability.

- Strong's Concordance for "Rock" (Hebrew: צוּר, tsur, H6697) refers to a large, immovable rock or cliff, symbolizing permanence and stability. The term is often used in a figurative sense to describe God's enduring faithfulness and protective nature.

Moses declares that God's work is perfect and His ways are just. The Rock imagery here signifies God's enduring righteousness and justice, making Him a reliable refuge for His people.

2. 1 Samuel 2:2:

- "There is none holy like the LORD, there is none besides you; there is no rock like our God" (ESV).

Hannah, in her prayer of thanksgiving, declares that there is no "rock" like God. This verse emphasizes the uniqueness of YHWH's strength and holiness. God is the only one who can provide unfailing support and protection, unlike the false gods of the surrounding nations.

- Strong's Concordance for "rock" (Hebrew: צוּר, tsur, H6697) maintains the same meaning—God is the immovable, unshakable refuge for His people.

3. 2 Samuel 22:32:

- "For who is God, besides the LORD? And who is a rock, besides our God?" (NASB).

David, in his song of deliverance, acknowledges that YHWH is the only true Rock. He contrasts YHWH with the false gods of the surrounding nations, asserting that only YHWH can be relied upon as a fortress and deliverer.

- The metaphor of "Rock" here again emphasizes God's exclusive ability to provide security, salvation, and protection.

4. Psalm 18:46:

- "The LORD lives! Blessed be my rock! And exalted be the God of my salvation" (ESV).

David praises God as "my rock" and the "God of my salvation." The Rock imagery here signifies YHWH's role as the one who saves and protects His people from their enemies. David often uses the Rock metaphor to express his complete dependence on God for deliverance and strength.

- Strong's Concordance for "rock" (Hebrew: צוּר, tsur, H6697) emphasizes strength, stability, and reliability, underscoring God's unwavering faithfulness in protecting His people.

In each of these Old Testament references, YHWH is called the Rock to emphasize His strength, steadfastness, and ability to protect and deliver His people. This metaphor portrays God as immovable and unchanging, qualities that are crucial for understanding God's nature and His relationship with Israel.

II. Christ as the Rock in the New Testament

1. 1 Corinthians 10:4:

- "And all drank the same spiritual drink. For they drank from the spiritual Rock that followed them, and the Rock was Christ" (ESV).

In this passage, the Apostle Paul identifies Christ as the Rock who followed and provided for the Israelites during their wilderness journey. Paul is referring to the events in Exodus 17:6, where Moses struck the rock at God's command, and water flowed out to quench the thirst of the people.

- Strong's Concordance for "Rock" (Greek: πέτρα, petra, G4073) refers to a massive rock or cliff. It symbolizes a solid, unshakable foundation.

By stating that "the Rock was Christ," Paul teaches that Jesus was the preexistent source of spiritual sustenance for Israel, even during the Exodus. Just as the physical rock provided life-sustaining water, Christ provides spiritual life and salvation to all who come to Him.

2. Exodus 17:6:

- "Behold, I will stand before you there on the rock at Horeb, and you shall strike the rock, and water will come out of it, that the people may drink" (ESV).

This passage recounts the event where Moses struck the rock at Horeb, and water miraculously flowed out to sustain the Israelites. The rock in this passage symbolizes Christ, who was "struck" at His crucifixion to bring spiritual life to humanity.

- The Strong's Concordance for "rock" in this passage (Hebrew: צוּר, tsur, H6697) once again points to a solid and stable rock. The imagery of the rock being struck and providing life-giving water foreshadows Christ's death and the life He gives through His sacrifice.

Paul's identification of Christ as the Rock in 1 Corinthians 10:4 ties together the Old and New Testament imagery. Just as YHWH was the Rock who sustained Israel in the wilderness, so Christ is the Rock who sustains believers today. This continuity between YHWH and Christ emphasizes Jesus' divinity and His eternal role in providing for God's people.

III. Theological Implications of Christ as the Rock

1. Christ's Eternal Nature:

- By identifying Christ as the Rock, Paul emphasizes that Jesus is the eternal, preexistent one who has always been involved in the salvation of His people. Christ's role as the Rock that followed the Israelites highlights His divinity and His eternal presence with His people.

2. Christ's Role as Provider and Sustainer:

- Just as the rock in the wilderness provided water to sustain the Israelites physically, Christ provides spiritual sustenance to His followers. Jesus is the source of living water, as He declares in John 4:14: "Whoever drinks the water I give them will never thirst" (NIV). Christ's provision of spiritual life is eternal, just as YHWH's protection of Israel was unchanging.

3. Christ's Identity as YHWH:

- The identification of Christ as the Rock in both the Old and New Testaments demonstrates the unity of the Godhead. Jesus is not a new revelation of God; He is the eternal God, YHWH, who has always been with His people. As YHWH is the Rock of Israel, so Jesus is the Rock of the Church.

IV. Conclusion

The metaphor of the Rock in Scripture is a profound representation of God's strength, faithfulness, and immutability. In the Old Testament, YHWH is repeatedly called the Rock who protected and sustained Israel. In the New Testament, Paul reveals that this Rock was Christ, showing that Jesus is the eternal God who has always been with His people, providing for them and sustaining them.

Understanding Christ as the Rock emphasizes His divinity and eternal nature. Just as YHWH was the immovable foundation for Israel, so Christ is the foundation of the Church. Jesus, as the Rock, is the source of salvation, protection, and spiritual life. To trust in Christ is to stand on an unshakable foundation, just as the Israelites trusted in YHWH as their Rock in the wilderness.

By linking the imagery of YHWH as the Rock with Christ as the Rock, the New Testament affirms the divine nature of Jesus and the continuity of God's plan of salvation through the ages. The Rock that followed the Israelites in the wilderness and provided for them is the same Rock that offers eternal life to all who believe in Him today.

CHAPTER 08

---

## THE DIVINE PREESENCE

*The Divine Presence of YHWH and Christ with the Israelites: A Study of Exodus 13:21 and 1 Corinthians 10:4*

The presence of God with His people during the Exodus is one of the most profound themes in the Bible, representing His guidance, protection, and provision. Exodus 13:21 reveals that YHWH (Yahweh) was present with the Israelites in the pillar of cloud by day and the pillar of fire by night. In the New Testament, the Apostle Paul, in 1 Corinthians 10:4, makes a striking connection by stating that Christ was the one who was present with the Israelites during their wilderness journey, describing Him as the spiritual Rock that followed them.

This chapter will provide a detailed expository study and comprehensive commentary on Exodus 13:21 and 1

Corinthians 10:4. We will analyze how the presence of YHWH in the Old Testament aligns with Paul's teaching that Christ was the divine figure accompanying Israel, using Strong's Concordance and cross-referencing other passages that help to illuminate this powerful truth.

I. YHWH in the Pillar of Cloud and Fire (Exodus 13:21)

1. Exodus 13:21:

- "And the LORD went before them by day in a pillar of cloud to lead them along the way, and by night in a pillar of fire to give them light, that they might travel by day and by night" (ESV).

In this passage, YHWH (Yahweh) manifests His presence in a visible and tangible way as He leads the Israelites out of Egypt and through the wilderness. The pillar of cloud by day and the pillar of fire by night served as a guide, protector, and assurance of God's constant presence with His people.

- Strong's Concordance for "pillar" (Hebrew: עַמּוּד, ammud, H5982) refers to a column or something that stands upright. This pillar is a physical manifestation of God's presence, a towering beacon that the Israelites could see as they traveled.

- "Cloud" (Hebrew: עָנָן, anan, H6051) is often used to represent God's presence in the Old Testament, as seen at Sinai when God descended in a cloud (Exodus 19:9, 24:15-18). The cloud symbolizes God's guidance and protection.

- "Fire" (Hebrew: אֵשׁ, esh, H784) represents God's holiness, presence, and purifying nature (cf. Exodus 3:2, Deuteronomy 4:24). The fire not only provided light for the Israelites but also symbolized God's power and protection.

This visible manifestation of YHWH's presence was crucial for the Israelites, as it demonstrated that God was with them in a personal and protective manner. The pillar of cloud and fire guided them safely through the desert and reassured them of YHWH's faithfulness.

II. Christ as the Divine Presence with Israel (1 Corinthians 10:4)

1. 1 Corinthians 10:4:

- "And all drank the same spiritual drink. For they drank from the spiritual Rock that followed them, and the Rock was Christ" (ESV).

In this verse, Paul is making an astonishing theological connection: he identifies Christ as the spiritual Rock who followed the Israelites during their wilderness journey. This statement builds on the earlier events in Exodus 17:6, where

Moses struck the rock and water flowed to quench the thirst of the people. Paul asserts that this Rock was a type of Christ, providing spiritual sustenance and foreshadowing Christ's role as the source of eternal life.

- Strong's Concordance for "Rock" (Greek: πέτρα, petra, G4073) refers to a large, immovable mass of rock, symbolizing stability and strength. In identifying Christ as the Rock, Paul emphasizes that Jesus was the spiritual source of sustenance, stability, and life for the Israelites.

- The phrase "spiritual drink" (Greek: πνευματικός πόμα, pneumatikos poma, G4152, G4221) refers to the supernatural sustenance provided by God, which Paul connects to Christ. Just as the Israelites received water from the rock in the desert, believers today receive spiritual sustenance from Christ, the Rock of our salvation.

Paul's identification of Christ as the spiritual Rock that "followed" the Israelites suggests that Christ was present with them throughout their journey, providing for their physical and spiritual needs. This further illustrates the continuity of God's presence from the Old Testament to the New Testament, with Christ being the embodiment of that divine presence.

III. Theological Implications of YHWH and Christ as the Divine Presence

1. Christ's Preexistence and Divinity:

- The connection between Exodus 13:21 and 1 Corinthians 10:4 highlights the preexistence of Christ. Just as YHWH was present with the Israelites in the pillar of cloud and fire, so too was Christ present with them as the spiritual Rock. This indicates that Christ, as the second person of the Trinity, has always been active in the history of salvation, even before His incarnation.

- In John 8:58, Jesus declares, "Before Abraham was, I am." This echoes YHWH's self-identification as "I AM" in Exodus 3:14, affirming Christ's eternal existence and divinity.

2. Christ as the Sustainer and Provider:

- Just as YHWH provided for the Israelites' physical needs during their journey through the wilderness, Christ provides for the spiritual needs of believers. In John 6:35, Jesus declares, "I am the bread of life; whoever comes to me shall not hunger, and whoever believes in me shall never thirst." This reinforces the imagery of Christ as the spiritual sustainer, just as He was the Rock providing water in the wilderness.

3. The Unity of the Godhead:

- The presence of YHWH in the Old Testament and Christ in the New Testament as the Rock illustrates the unity of the Godhead. Although YHWH and Christ are distinct persons, they are one in essence and purpose, both acting as the protector, guide, and sustainer of God's people. This unity is further demonstrated in John 10:30, where Jesus states, "I and the Father are one."

4. The Divine Guidance and Protection:

- The pillar of cloud and fire that accompanied the Israelites through the wilderness symbolizes God's guidance and protection. Christ's role as the spiritual Rock also points to His ongoing guidance and protection of believers. In Matthew 28:20, Jesus promises, "And behold, I am with you always, to the end of the age." Just as YHWH was with the Israelites, Christ is with His Church, leading and protecting them.

IV. Other Scriptural Connections

1. Psalm 78:14-16:

- "In the daytime he led them with a cloud, and all the night with a fiery light. He split rocks in the wilderness and gave them drink abundantly as from the deep. He made streams come out of the rock and caused waters to flow down like rivers" (ESV).

This psalm recounts YHWH's provision and guidance during the Exodus, highlighting both the pillar of cloud and fire and the miraculous provision of water from the rock. It points forward to Christ as the Rock who would provide spiritual nourishment to His people.

2. John 7:37-38:

- "If anyone thirsts, let him come to me and drink. Whoever believes in me, as the Scripture has said, 'Out of his heart will flow rivers of living water.'"

Here, Jesus invites believers to come to Him for spiritual sustenance, drawing on the imagery of water flowing from the rock in the wilderness. Christ, as the source of living water, continues to provide for His people's spiritual needs.

V. Conclusion

In Exodus 13:21, YHWH is revealed as the one who led the Israelites through the wilderness in the pillar of cloud and fire, providing both guidance and protection. In the New Testament, 1 Corinthians 10:4 reveals that Christ, the preexistent Son of God, was also present with the Israelites as the spiritual Rock who sustained them. This continuity between YHWH's presence in the Old Testament and Christ's presence in the New Testament underscores the unity of the Godhead and the eternal role of Christ in the history of salvation.

Understanding Christ as the Rock and the divine presence with Israel enriches our comprehension of His preexistence, divinity, and His ongoing role as the sustainer and provider for His people. Just as YHWH was the refuge and guide for the Israelites, so too is Christ the Rock of our salvation, leading us on our spiritual journey and providing us with eternal life.

CHAPTER 09

---

## THE DIVINE CREATOR

*The Divine Creator: YHWH and Christ in Psalm 102 and Hebrews 1*

The identity of Christ as the divine Creator is a central theme in the New Testament, and it is deeply rooted in Old Testament scripture. Psalm 102 is a powerful reflection on the eternal nature of YHWH (Yahweh) and His role as the Creator of the heavens and the earth. However, the author of Hebrews directly applies this psalm to Jesus, thus affirming His divine nature and role as the Creator. This connection between Psalm 102 and Hebrews 1 reveals Christ's eternal existence and His participation in the work of creation.

This chapter will explore Psalm 102:25-27 and Hebrews 1:8-12 in an expository and comprehensive commentary, integrating the use of Strong's Concordance to provide deeper insight into the meaning of key words and concepts. By understanding the context and theology behind these passages, we will see how Christ is rightly recognized as the divine Creator alongside YHWH.

I. Psalm 102: YHWH as the Eternal Creator

1. Psalm 102:25-27:

- "Of old you laid the foundation of the earth, and the heavens are the work of your hands. They will perish, but you will remain; they will all wear out like a garment. You will change them like a robe, and they will pass away, but you are the same, and your years have no end." (ESV)

In this passage, the psalmist extols YHWH as the eternal Creator, contrasting the temporal nature of creation with the unchanging nature of God. The earth and heavens—no matter how vast and majestic—will one day perish and be renewed, but YHWH remains forever. This declaration emphasizes YHWH's sovereignty and eternal nature.

- Strong's Concordance for "laid the foundation" (Hebrew: יָסַד, yasad, H3245) means to establish or fix firmly. This indicates that YHWH is the one who fixed the earth in its place, firmly establishing the universe by His power.

- "Work of your hands" (Hebrew: מַעֲשֵׂה, maaseh, H4639) refers to God's craftsmanship. The heavens are described as God's handiwork, emphasizing the intentional and personal nature of His creative acts.

- "They will perish" (Hebrew: אָבַד, abad, H6) means to be destroyed or come to an end. This is a reference to the temporal nature of the created order, which contrasts with YHWH's eternal and unchanging nature.

This passage paints a picture of YHWH as the Creator who stands outside of time and remains eternally the same, even as creation itself ages and decays. The psalmist presents YHWH as the everlasting God, whose years have no end, a truth that is affirmed repeatedly throughout the Bible.

II. Hebrews 1: The Application of Psalm 102 to Christ

1. Hebrews 1:8-12:

- "But of the Son he says, 'Your throne, O God, is forever and ever, the scepter of uprightness is the scepter of your kingdom. You have loved righteousness and hated wickedness; therefore God, your God, has anointed you with the oil of gladness beyond your companions.' And, 'You, Lord, laid the foundation of the earth in the beginning, and the heavens are the work of your hands; they will perish, but you remain; they will all wear out like a garment, like a robe you will roll them up, like a garment they will be changed. But you are the same, and your years will have no end.'" (ESV)

In this passage, the author of Hebrews applies Psalm 102 directly to Christ. By doing so, the writer affirms that Christ, like YHWH, is the eternal Creator who laid the foundations of the earth and whose existence transcends time.

- Strong's Concordance for "throne" (Greek: θρόνος, thronos, G2362) refers to a seat of power and authority, symbolizing Christ's reign as King and Judge. His throne is described as eternal, emphasizing His divine kingship.

- "Lord" (Greek: Κύριε, kurie, G2962) is a term used to denote supreme authority. In applying this title to Christ, the Hebrews writer affirms that Jesus holds the same divine status as YHWH.

- "Laid the foundation" (Greek: θεμελιόω, themelioo, G2311) carries the same meaning as in Psalm 102—referring to the act of establishing or fixing firmly the earth. By attributing this act to Christ, the Hebrews writer affirms that Jesus was the agent of creation, a truth echoed in John 1:3 ("All things were made through him").

The application of Psalm 102 to Jesus in Hebrews 1 presents a strong theological claim: Christ is not only the promised Messiah but also shares in the divine nature of YHWH, as evidenced by His role in creation. This passage demonstrates that the Son is both eternal and sovereign, possessing the attributes of God Himself.

III. The Unity of YHWH and Christ as Creator

The link between Psalm 102 and Hebrews 1 provides a clear biblical affirmation of Christ's divinity. The New Testament writer takes a passage originally speaking about YHWH and applies it directly to Jesus, illustrating the deep connection between the Father and the Son in their role as Creator.

1. Christ as Creator:

- The New Testament repeatedly affirms Christ's role in creation, emphasizing that He is not merely a created being but the Creator Himself. In Colossians 1:16, Paul writes, "For by him all things were created, in heaven and on earth, visible and invisible, whether thrones or dominions or rulers or authorities—all things were created through him and for him."

- Likewise, in John 1:1-3, Christ is described as the Word (Greek: Λόγος, Logos, G3056) who was with God in the beginning and through whom all things were made. This reinforces the idea that Christ, like YHWH, is the divine Creator.

2. The Eternal Nature of Christ:

- Just as Psalm 102 speaks of YHWH's eternal existence, the New Testament reveals that Christ also possesses this eternal nature. In John 8:58, Jesus declares, "Before Abraham was, I am." This statement not only affirms Christ's preexistence but also connects Him to the divine name revealed to Moses in Exodus 3:14.

- In Revelation 1:8, Jesus is described as the "Alpha and the Omega," the one "who is and who was and who is to come, the Almighty." This title echoes the eternal nature of YHWH in the Old Testament and applies it to Christ.

IV. Theological Implications

1. Christ's Divinity and Eternality:

- The application of Psalm 102 to Christ in Hebrews 1 underscores the belief that Jesus is divine and eternal. He shares the same attributes as YHWH, including immutability (unchangeableness) and sovereignty over creation. This challenges any notion of Christ as a mere created being and places Him firmly within the Godhead.

2. The Continuity of Scripture:

- The use of Old Testament passages to describe Christ in the New Testament reveals the deep continuity between the Hebrew Scriptures and the Christian faith. The same God who revealed Himself as YHWH to the Israelites is now revealed as Jesus Christ, the Son of God.

3. The Role of Christ in Salvation History:

- As both the Creator and Sustainer of the universe, Christ's role in salvation history is unparalleled. He is the one who brought all things into existence, and He is the one who will ultimately renew and redeem creation. In Revelation 21:5, Jesus declares, "Behold, I am making all things new." Just as the heavens and the earth will perish, they will also be renewed through Christ.

V. Other Scriptural Connections

1. Isaiah 45:12:

- "I made the earth and created man on it; it was my hands that stretched out the heavens, and I commanded all their host."

This verse speaks of YHWH's role as the Creator, paralleling the descriptions of Christ's creative work in the New Testament.

2. Psalm 33:6:

- "By the word of the LORD the heavens were made, and by the breath of his mouth all their host."

This passage emphasizes the power of God's Word in creation, which is later applied to Christ in John 1:1.

The connection between Psalm 102 and Hebrews 1 provides powerful biblical evidence that Jesus Christ shares the divine nature and eternal attributes of YHWH. By applying a passage that originally speaks about YHWH's role as the Creator and Sustainer of the universe directly to Christ, the writer of Hebrews makes an unambiguous declaration of Christ's divinity and His participation in creation.

The fact that YHWH is called the Creator in Psalm 102, yet the same role is attributed to Jesus in Hebrews 1, emphasizes the unity and equality between the Father and the Son. This unity does not erase their distinct persons within the Trinity, but rather highlights that both share in the divine identity and purpose. Christ is not a mere intermediary or created being; He is fully divine, existing eternally with the Father and possessing the authority to create, sustain, and renew the world.

Furthermore, the imagery of creation "perishing like a garment" but God and Christ "remaining the same" (Hebrews 1:12) speaks to the enduring sovereignty of both. Creation is transient and subject to decay, but God, in His eternal power, will remain unchanging, and the same can be said of Christ. This reinforces the biblical teaching that Jesus is not only the promised Messiah but also the eternal Creator who transcends time and space.

The Eternal Creator: Christ's Preeminence

1. Christ as the Eternal Creator:

The identification of Christ as the Creator is reinforced throughout the New Testament. Colossians 1:16-17 proclaims, "For by him all things were created, in heaven and on earth, visible and invisible…all things were created through him and for him. And he is before all things, and in him all things hold together." These verses align perfectly with the message of Psalm 102 and Hebrews 1, where Christ is depicted as the one who laid the foundation of the earth, and in whose hands the entire creation rests.

Christ's preexistence and active role in creation affirm His supremacy over all things. He is the source of all life and existence, which is not only an affirmation of His divinity but also an essential truth for Christian faith. The Creator is worthy of worship and allegiance, and by identifying Jesus as the Creator, the New Testament invites believers to worship Him as YHWH.

2. Christ's Unchanging Nature:

Another significant implication of these passages is the assertion that Christ is eternal and unchanging. Just as Psalm 102:27 declares that "You are the same, and your years will have no end," the writer of Hebrews 13:8 states, "Jesus Christ is the same yesterday and today and forever." This consistency and permanence highlight Christ's divine nature.

He is not subject to the limitations of time and decay, and His eternal nature provides believers with the assurance that His power and love will never wane or diminish.

Christ's Role in the New Creation

While Psalm 102 and Hebrews 1 emphasize Christ's role in the original creation, the New Testament also reveals that He will play a central role in the new creation. In Revelation 21:5, Christ declares, "Behold, I am making all things new." Just as He created the world in the beginning, He will also bring about the renewal of all creation in the eschatological future. This truth connects to the idea in Psalm 102 that the old creation will "wear out like a garment," but God will bring about its renewal.

Through His death and resurrection, Christ has already begun the work of the new creation in the hearts of believers (2 Corinthians 5:17), and one day, He will complete this work by renewing the heavens and the earth (Revelation 21:1). Thus, Christ is not only the Creator of the past but also the Creator of the future.

Final Reflections

The unity of YHWH and Christ as the Creator provides a profound insight into the nature of God. The Scriptures present Jesus as more than a teacher or prophet; He is the eternal Son of God, coequal with the Father, and fully involved in the work of creation, sustenance, and renewal. Recognizing Jesus as the Creator and the eternal "I AM" leads to a deeper understanding of His divine identity and calls for a response of worship and reverence.

This truth has direct implications for Christian faith and theology. Acknowledging Christ's divine role as the Creator establishes Him as the object of our faith, the foundation of our existence, and the hope for the renewal of all things. As Hebrews 1:3 declares, "He upholds the universe by the word of his power," a statement that gives Christians confidence that, in Christ, their lives and futures are secure in the hands of the eternal and unchanging God.

Summary

- Psalm 102 speaks of YHWH as the eternal Creator who laid the foundations of the earth and will outlast creation itself.

- Hebrews 1 applies this description of YHWH directly to Christ, revealing Him as the divine, eternal Creator.

- Strong's Concordance highlights key terms such as "foundation," "work," and "perish," deepening our understanding of Christ's role as the Creator and Sustainer.

- The New Testament consistently portrays Christ as the Creator of all things, eternal and unchanging.

- This truth calls believers to worship Christ as the divine Creator and to trust in His eternal power and authority over all creation, both now and in the future.

Christ is "the same yesterday and today and forever" (Hebrews 13:8), and in Him, we find our eternal hope, not only in this life but in the new creation to come.

CHAPTER 10

---

## ISAIAH'S VISION OF YHWH AND JESUS' GLORY

*The Vision of Isaiah and the Revelation of Jesus*

In Isaiah 6:5, the prophet Isaiah recounts a profound vision where he sees YHWH seated on His throne in glory: "Woe is me! For I am undone; because I am a man of unclean lips, and I dwell in the midst of a people of unclean lips: for mine eyes have seen the King, the Lord of hosts." This passage is pivotal because it raises an important theological question: How could Isaiah, a man, see YHWH, when Scripture asserts that no one has seen God (the Father)? John 1:18 declares, "No man hath seen God at any time, the only begotten Son, which is in the bosom of the Father, he hath declared him." Additionally, 1 John 4:12 repeats, "No man hath seen God at any time."

The resolution to this seeming contradiction comes in John 12:41, where the apostle John interprets Isaiah's vision. Speaking of the unbelief of the Jewish leaders, John writes: "These things said Isaiah, when he saw His glory, and spake of Him." Here, John identifies that Isaiah, in his vision of YHWH, actually saw Jesus Christ in His pre-incarnate glory. This insight bridges the Old and New Testaments, revealing that the One Isaiah saw was indeed the eternal Son, who shares the glory of the Father.

In this expository study, we will explore the vision of Isaiah in Isaiah 6, analyze how it connects to the revelation of Jesus Christ in John 12, and examine the theological implications of Jesus' divine glory, using Strong's Concordance for a deeper word study.

Part 1: Isaiah's Vision of YHWH (Isaiah 6:1-5)

Isaiah's Vision: "I Saw the Lord"

In Isaiah 6:1, the prophet describes a remarkable experience: "In the year that king Uzziah died I saw also the Lord sitting upon a throne, high and lifted up, and his train filled the temple." The Hebrew word used for "Lord" here is אֲדֹנָי (Adonai), which emphasizes God's sovereign rulership and majesty. Isaiah is overwhelmed by the holiness and majesty of YHWH, and the seraphim surrounding the throne call out, "Holy, holy, holy is the Lord of hosts: the whole earth is full of his glory" (Isaiah 6:3).

Isaiah responds with humility and fear, saying, "Woe is me! For I am undone; because I am a man of unclean lips" (Isaiah 6:5). His reaction to seeing YHWH reveals the overwhelming reality of God's holiness and the prophet's sense of personal unworthiness.

Strong's Concordance Word Study:

- "Lord" (Adonai – H136): This name emphasizes God as the sovereign ruler. Isaiah acknowledges that he is in the presence of the supreme King, who holds absolute authority over creation.

- "Glory" (Kabod – H3519): The word "glory" refers to the weightiness and splendor of God's divine presence, filling the temple and the earth.

Part 2: No Man Has Seen God (John 1:18; 1 John 4:12)

The Father's Invisibility:

Scripture consistently teaches that God the Father, in His essence, is invisible and transcendent. John 1:18 states: "No man hath seen God at any time; the only begotten Son, who is in the bosom of the Father, He hath declared Him." This passage clarifies that it is through Jesus, the Son, that we come to know God. Jesus, as the "image of the invisible God" (Colossians 1:15), is the One who reveals the Father to humanity.

Similarly, 1 John 4:12 reinforces this idea: "No man hath seen God at any time. If we love one another, God dwelleth in us, and His love is perfected in us." The apostle John emphasizes the invisible nature of the Father, but this does not preclude the revelation of God through the Son.

Strong's Concordance Word Study:

- "Seen" (Horao – G3708): This Greek verb means to perceive with the eyes, to discern, or to understand. The assertion that no one has "seen" God emphasizes that no one has fully perceived or comprehended God in His essence apart from the revelation through the Son.

Part 3: John's Revelation of Jesus' Glory (John 12:41)

Isaiah Saw Jesus' Glory:

The key to understanding Isaiah's vision in light of New Testament revelation comes in John 12:41, where John writes, "These things said Isaiah, when he saw His glory, and spake of Him." In this context, John refers to Isaiah 6, affirming that the glory Isaiah saw in the temple was, in fact, the pre-incarnate glory of Jesus Christ.

This is a profound statement about Christ's deity and pre-existence. Jesus did not simply come into being at His incarnation; He existed eternally with the Father and was actively involved in revealing the divine presence throughout the Old Testament. Isaiah's vision of YHWH was thus a vision of Jesus, the eternal Word of God.

The Glory of Christ in the Old Testament:

Jesus' glory is not limited to His earthly ministry but is seen throughout Scripture. In John 17:5, Jesus prays to the Father, saying, "And now, O Father, glorify Me together with Yourself, with the glory which I had with You before the world was." This underscores that Christ shared in the divine glory from eternity past. The vision of Isaiah is one manifestation of that glory, seen by the prophet as a foreshadowing of Christ's coming.

Strong's Concordance Word Study:

- "Glory" (Doxa – G1391): In Greek, "glory" refers to honor, splendor, or divine radiance. The glory that Isaiah saw was the divine radiance of Christ, which John identifies as the same glory that Jesus possessed with the Father before the world began.

Part 4: The Implications of Christ's Divinity

Christ as YHWH:

By linking Isaiah 6 with John 12:41, the Bible reveals that Jesus shares the divine name and identity of YHWH. The vision of Isaiah 6 is not just a vision of a majestic king but a revelation of the Second Person of the Trinity, the Son of God, who existed before all time and who participated in the divine work of creation and redemption. The seraphim's thrice-repeated cry of "Holy, holy, holy" in Isaiah's vision may also allude to the Trinitarian nature of God.

Jesus Reveals the Father:

Though no one has seen the Father, Jesus reveals Him. In John 14:9, Jesus tells Philip, "He that hath seen Me hath seen the Father." This statement does not mean that Jesus and the Father are the same person, but that to see Jesus is to see the full revelation of God's character and nature. Jesus is the "image of the invisible God" (Colossians 1:15), and through Him, the Father is made known.

Jesus, the Revealer of YHWH's Glory

Isaiah's vision of YHWH in Isaiah 6 is a profound revelation of the divine glory, which the New Testament identifies as the glory of Jesus Christ. While no one has seen the Father in His full essence, Jesus, as the eternal Son, reveals God to humanity. John 12:41 affirms that the glory Isaiah saw was none other than the pre-incarnate glory of Christ, establishing His divinity and eternal existence.

Jesus is YHWH in the sense that He shares the divine name, glory, and attributes of the God of Israel. He is distinct from the Father, yet fully one with Him in essence and purpose. As the eternal "I AM" (John 8:58), Jesus stands as the visible manifestation of the invisible God, the One through whom all things were made, and the One who reveals the Father's glory to the world.

Understanding Jesus' divine glory as revealed in the Old Testament deepens our worship and appreciation of who He is: the eternal Son of God, the radiance of God's glory, and the exact representation of His being (Hebrews 1:3). Just as Isaiah was overwhelmed by the holiness of YHWH, we too are called to stand in awe of the majesty and glory of Jesus Christ, our Lord and Savior.

CHAPTER 11

## CHRIST AS "EMMANUEL" – GOD WITH US

*The Meaning of Emmanuel*

The name Emmanuel, which means "God with us," reveals a profound truth about the identity and mission of Jesus Christ. This name, given to Jesus in prophecy and later applied to Him at His birth, encapsulates the mystery of the incarnation—that God Himself became flesh and dwelt among humanity. In Isaiah 7:14, the prophet foretells: "Therefore the Lord himself shall give you a sign; Behold, a virgin shall conceive, and bear a son, and shall call his name Emmanuel." This prophecy finds its ultimate fulfillment in Matthew 1:23, where the angel announces to Joseph the birth of Jesus, quoting Isaiah's prophecy directly: "Behold, a virgin shall be with child, and shall bring forth a son, and they shall call his name Emmanuel, which being interpreted is, God with us."

Throughout the New Testament, Jesus is consistently identified as God—not just a godly man, teacher, or prophet, but God in the flesh, coequal with the Father. From the prologue of John's Gospel, where Jesus is called "the Word, who was with God and was God" (John 1:1), to the declaration of Thomas, who worships Him as "My Lord and my God" (John 20:28), the New Testament consistently affirms the full deity of Christ. This chapter will provide an expository study of these key passages, using Strong's Concordance for a deeper understanding of the terms used to describe Christ's divinity.

Part 1: The Prophecy of Emmanuel (Isaiah 7:14)

Isaiah 7:14 and Its Fulfillment in Matthew 1:23

The name Emmanuel appears first in Isaiah 7:14, where God promises a miraculous sign to the house of David. This sign—a virgin conceiving and bearing a son—is a divine intervention meant to confirm God's presence and faithfulness to His people. In the context of Isaiah's day, the prophecy had an immediate application, but the ultimate fulfillment comes in the birth of Jesus, the true Emmanuel.

When Matthew 1:23 quotes Isaiah's prophecy, it does so to affirm that Jesus is not just another prophet or teacher, but God Himself come to dwell among humanity. Jesus is literally "God with us", making His incarnation a manifestation of God's presence in a way that had never occurred before.

Strong's Concordance Word Study:

- "Emmanuel" (Immanu El – H6005): This Hebrew term is a compound word meaning "with us is God." It highlights the presence of God in a personal, relational way. The word "El" refers to God, while "Immanu" means "with us." The name underscores the reality of God's presence in Jesus, who is both fully human and fully divine.

Part 2: Jesus as the Word and God (John 1:1, 14)

The Logos: The Eternal Word

In the opening verse of John's Gospel, we encounter one of the most profound theological statements in the New Testament: "In the beginning was the Word, and the Word was with God, and the Word was God" (John 1:1). The Word (Greek: Logos) is identified as both eternal and divine, existing before all creation. The Logos is not a created being but shares the same nature and essence as God.

In John 1:14, John clarifies the identity of the Logos: "And the Word was made flesh, and dwelt among us, (and we beheld His glory, the glory as of the only begotten of the Father,) full of grace and truth." The Logos—the eternal Word—became flesh in the person of Jesus Christ. This is the mystery of the incarnation: God Himself took on human nature and lived among His people.

Strong's Concordance Word Study:

- "Word" (Logos – G3056): This Greek term can mean "speech," "reason," or "divine expression." In the context of John 1, the Logos is the preexistent Christ, who is both distinct from the Father (as the Word was with God) and fully divine (the Word was God).

- "Dwelt" (Skenoo – G4637): This term means to "tabernacle" or "dwell in a tent." It evokes the image of God's presence in the tabernacle in the wilderness (Exodus 40:34-35), now realized in the person of Jesus Christ, who dwells among His people.

Part 3: Jesus Worshiped as God (John 20:28; Acts 20:28)

homas's Confession: "My Lord and My God"

One of the clearest confessions of Christ's divinity comes from the apostle Thomas after Jesus' resurrection. In John 20:28, Thomas, upon seeing the risen Christ, exclaims, "My Lord and my God!" This is not just an expression of amazement; it is a declaration of Jesus' divine identity. Thomas recognizes that Jesus is more than a man—He is the Lord and God, deserving of worship and reverence.

Christ's Divinity in the Early Church (Acts 20:28)

In Acts 20:28, the apostle Paul instructs the Ephesian elders: "Take heed therefore unto yourselves, and to all the flock, over the which the Holy Ghost hath made you overseers, to feed the church of God, which He hath purchased with His own blood." Here, Paul makes a remarkable statement about the nature of Jesus. He refers to the church as the "church of God," which was purchased "with His own blood." This identification of Jesus as God is striking, as it links the divine nature of God with the sacrificial death of Christ.

Strong's Concordance Word Study:

- "God" (Theos – G2316): This Greek term is used throughout the New Testament to refer to the one true God. In both John 20:28 and Acts 20:28, it is applied directly to Jesus, affirming His deity.

- "Lord" (Kurios – G2962): This title means "master" or "sovereign." In the context of John 20:28, it is a recognition of Jesus' divine authority and status.

Part 4: Paul's Testimony to Christ's Deity (Romans 9:5; Titus 2:13)

Christ: God Over All (Romans 9:5)

In Romans 9:5, Paul writes concerning Christ: "Whose are the fathers, and of whom as concerning the flesh

Christ came, who is over all, God blessed forever. Amen." In this verse, Paul identifies Jesus as the one "who is over all" and describes Him as "God blessed forever." This statement affirms the supreme authority and eternal nature of Christ, underscoring His divinity.

Our Great God and Savior (Titus 2:13)

In Titus 2:13, Paul describes the anticipation of Christ's return: "Looking for that blessed hope, and the glorious appearing of the great God and our Savior Jesus Christ." Here, Paul explicitly refers to Jesus as both "God" and "Savior." The construction of the Greek text indicates that "the great God" and "our Savior" both refer to the same person—Jesus Christ.

Strong's Concordance Word Study:

- "Savior" (Soter – G4990): This Greek word means "deliverer" or "preserver." In the New Testament, it is often used to describe Jesus, who saves His people from their sins.

Part 5: Christ as God in Hebrews 1:8-12

The Son as God (Hebrews 1:8-9)

In Hebrews 1:8-9, the writer applies a passage from Psalm 45:6-7 to Jesus, affirming His divine kingship: "But unto the Son He saith, Thy throne, O God, is forever and ever: a scepter of righteousness is the scepter of Thy kingdom.

Thou hast loved righteousness, and hated iniquity; therefore God, even thy God, hath anointed Thee with the oil of gladness above Thy fellows." Here, the Son is directly addressed as "God," emphasizing His eternal reign and righteous character.

Jesus as Creator (Hebrews 1:10-12)

The writer continues by applying Psalm 102:25-27 to Jesus: "And, Thou, Lord, in the beginning hast laid the foundation of the earth; and the heavens are the works of thine hands: They shall perish; but thou remainest; and they all shall wax old as doth a garment." This passage identifies Jesus as the Creator and sustainer of the universe, further underscoring His divine nature.

Christ, Emmanuel—God With Us

The biblical evidence for the divinity of Christ is overwhelming. From the prophecy of Isaiah 7:14, where He is called Emmanuel ("God with us"), to the declarations of the New Testament that Jesus is God in the flesh, the Scriptures consistently affirm that Jesus is not merely a human teacher, prophet, or moral leader, but truly God incarnate. The title of Emmanuel holds deep theological significance, as it encapsulates the mystery of the incarnation—God choosing to dwell among humanity in the person of Jesus Christ.

Through the study of the Strong's Concordance and an expository analysis of key passages, we have seen how the New Testament writers present Jesus as equal with God, sharing the same nature and attributes as the Father. In John 1:1, Jesus is identified as the eternal Logos, who was with God and was God. In John 1:14, we are told that the Word became flesh and dwelt among us, revealing the glory of God in a way that was accessible to human beings.

Moreover, the worship of Jesus as God throughout the New Testament confirms that His divinity was recognized by His followers. When Thomas confessed, "My Lord and my God" in John 20:28, he was acknowledging the full reality of who Jesus is—the risen Lord who shares in the divine nature. Paul also explicitly refers to Christ as God in passages like Romans 9:5 and Titus 2:13, where he calls Jesus "God over all" and "our great God and Savior."

The application of Old Testament passages, originally referring to YHWH (Jehovah), to Jesus further reinforces this truth. In Psalm 102, YHWH is described as the one who laid the foundations of the earth, but the writer of Hebrews applies this directly to Christ (Hebrews 1:8-12), showing that Jesus is the Creator and sustainer of all things, just as YHWH is. Likewise, Isaiah's vision in Isaiah 6 is interpreted by John as a vision of Jesus' glory (John 12:41), affirming that the YHWH whom Isaiah saw was none other than the pre-incarnate Christ.

The doctrine of the Trinity is crucial for understanding how Jesus can be both Emmanuel—God with us—and distinct from the Father. Jesus is not the Father, but He is fully God, coequal and coeternal with the Father and the Holy Spirit. This is why Jesus could claim, "Before Abraham was, I AM" (John 8:58), identifying Himself with the divine name YHWH, and why He could forgive sins, a prerogative reserved for God alone (Mark 2:5-7).

In summary, Jesus is truly Emmanuel—God with us. His incarnation reveals the depth of God's love and the extent to which God was willing to go to redeem humanity. By becoming human, Jesus entered into our world, experienced our sufferings, and provided the perfect sacrifice for our sins. Yet, He remains fully divine, worthy of worship, and the eternal Word who upholds all things. The name Emmanuel assures us that God is not distant or detached but intimately involved in the lives of His people through the person of Jesus Christ. In Him, we find the fullness of God's grace and truth, and through Him, we have access to eternal life.

Key Takeaways:

1. Emmanuel (God with us): Jesus is the fulfillment of the prophecy in Isaiah 7:14; His birth is the literal manifestation of God's presence among His people.

2. Jesus as the Word (Logos): In John 1:1, 14, Jesus is identified as the eternal Word, fully divine, and the one who took on human nature.

3. Jesus worshiped as God: The worship of Jesus as God in John 20:28 and the application of Old Testament YHWH passages to Him in the New Testament affirm His deity.

4. Paul's testimony to Christ's divinity: Paul calls Jesus God in passages like Romans 9:5 and Titus 2:13, showing that early Christians understood and worshiped Jesus as divine.

5. The doctrine of the Trinity: While Jesus is distinct from the Father, He is fully God, coequal and coeternal with the Father and the Holy Spirit, making Him the true Emmanuel—God with us.

In light of these truths, believers are called to worship Jesus as Lord and God, acknowledging His divine nature and His redemptive work on our behalf. Through faith in Him, we are brought into fellowship with God, who, in Christ, is truly with us.

# CHAPTER 12

# THE STENE STUMBLING AND THE ROCK OF OFFENSE

*YHWH and Jesus*

The concept of a "stone of stumbling" and a "rock of offense" is a powerful and vivid metaphor that is deeply rooted in both the Old and New Testaments. In Isaiah 8:13-14, YHWH is described as this stone, which would become a source of stumbling for those who reject Him. The apostle Paul, however, directly applies this prophetic imagery to Jesus Christ in Romans 9:33 and alludes to it in Romans 10:9-11. This application of an Old Testament description of YHWH to Jesus serves as another significant affirmation of Christ's divinity and the unique nature of His mission.

This chapter will explore how these passages are interconnected, how Paul uses them to emphasize the nature of faith and unbelief, and how Strong's Concordance further illuminates the meaning of key terms. We will also examine the broader theological implications of Jesus as the "stone of stumbling" and how this metaphor relates to both salvation and judgment.

The Old Testament Context: YHWH as the Stone of Stumbling

In Isaiah 8:13-14, the prophet Isaiah speaks of the Lord (YHWH) as both a sanctuary and a stumbling block:

> "Sanctify the LORD of hosts Himself; and let Him be your fear, and let Him be your dread. And He shall be for a sanctuary; but for a stone of stumbling and for a rock of offense to both the houses of Israel, for a gin and for a snare to the inhabitants of Jerusalem." (Isaiah 8:13-14, KJV)

Here, the "LORD of hosts" (YHWH) is described as a sanctuary, a place of refuge for those who trust in Him, but also as a stone of stumbling and a rock of offense for those who reject Him. The same God who offers protection to those who honor Him becomes an obstacle and a source of judgment to those who fail to recognize Him. This dual function of YHWH as both refuge and stumbling block is a central theme in Isaiah's prophecy, pointing to how Israel's response to God's self-revelation would lead to either salvation or ruin.

Key Words from Strong's Concordance:

- Sanctuary (H4720, מִקְדָּשׁ): Refers to a sacred place, or a holy place of refuge, indicating God's role as a place of protection and holiness for His people.

- Stumbling (H4383, מִכְשׁוֹל): Refers to an obstacle or something that causes one to fall. In this context, YHWH becomes a stumbling block to those who reject Him.

- Offense (H5061, נֶגֶף): Refers to something that causes one to take offense or become a trap or snare. This further emphasizes the nature of YHWH as a cause of judgment for the disobedient.

Paul's Application of Isaiah's Prophecy to Christ

In the New Testament, the apostle Paul draws directly from this imagery in Romans 9:32-33:

> "Wherefore? Because they sought it not by faith, but as it were by the works of the law. For they stumbled at that stumblingstone; as it is written, Behold, I lay in Zion a stumblingstone and rock of offense: and whosoever believeth on him shall not be ashamed." (Romans 9:32-33, KJV)

Paul applies the language of Isaiah's prophecy to Jesus Christ, presenting Him as the stumbling stone for Israel. The Jewish people, seeking righteousness through the works of the law, stumbled over Jesus, who came not to abolish the law but to fulfill it. Paul's argument is that they failed to recognize Christ as the Messiah because they sought righteousness through their own efforts rather than through faith in Him. In doing so, they stumbled over the very one who was meant to be their salvation.

Paul's use of Isaiah 8:14 in this context reinforces the idea that Jesus, like YHWH in the Old Testament, serves both as a source of salvation for those who believe and as a stumbling block for those who reject Him.

Key Words from Strong's Concordance:

- Stumblingstone (G4348, προσκομμα): Refers to something that causes one to stumble or fall. Jesus is the stumbling stone for those who seek righteousness by works.

- Rock of offense (G4625, σκανδαλον): This word means a trap or snare, and in a figurative sense, it refers to something that causes spiritual downfall. Jesus became this for the unbelieving Jews.

- Ashamed (G2617, καταισχύνω): To be dishonored or put to shame. Paul declares that those who believe in Christ will not be ashamed, referencing Isaiah 28:16, where belief in God's cornerstone brings security and salvation.

Paul echoes this same theme in Romans 10:9-11, where he explains that confessing Jesus as Lord and believing in His resurrection leads to salvation:

> "...if thou shalt confess with thy mouth the Lord Jesus, and shalt believe in thine heart that God hath raised Him from the dead, thou shalt be saved. For with the heart man believeth unto righteousness; and with the mouth confession is made unto salvation. For the Scripture saith, Whosoever believeth on Him shall not be ashamed." (Romans 10:9-11, KJV)

Theological Implications: Jesus as the Stone of Stumbling

The imagery of the stone of stumbling and the rock of offense carries deep theological significance. It speaks to the paradox of Christ's mission: He is the cornerstone of salvation for those who believe, yet He becomes an obstacle for those who rely on their own righteousness. The metaphor illustrates the radical nature of the gospel, which confronts human pride and self-reliance, demanding faith and humility in accepting God's way of salvation.

Christ as the Cornerstone:

- 1 Peter 2:6-8: Peter similarly applies Isaiah 28:16 and Isaiah 8:14 to Christ, describing Him as the chief cornerstone—the foundation of God's people—and simultaneously a stone of stumbling for the disobedient.

- Ephesians 2:20: Paul also identifies Jesus as the chief cornerstone, upon which the household of God is built, with the apostles and prophets forming the rest of the foundation.

Jesus' role as the cornerstone is inseparable from His identity as God incarnate. The stone of stumbling and rock of offense metaphor emphasizes that it is impossible to approach God apart from Christ. He is the dividing line between those who are saved and those who are condemned. As Isaiah 28:16 affirms, those who put their faith in this cornerstone will not be put to shame, but those who reject Him will stumble and fall.

Christ, the Stone of Stumbling and the Rock of Offense

The prophetic imagery of YHWH as the stone of stumbling in Isaiah 8:13-14 is fulfilled in Jesus Christ, as Paul reveals in Romans 9:32-33. Just as YHWH was a sanctuary and a source of judgment for Israel, so too is Christ for all who encounter Him. For those who believe, He is the cornerstone of salvation, but for those who reject Him, He becomes a stumbling block that leads to their spiritual ruin.

Through an exhaustive study of the Strong's Concordance and a close examination of the relevant passages, we see that the stone of stumbling metaphor is central to understanding the nature of faith in Christ. It highlights the exclusive nature of salvation through Jesus and underscores the necessity of approaching God on His terms, through faith, rather than through self-reliance or works.

In the end, this metaphor challenges each of us to reflect on how we approach Christ. Will He be for us the cornerstone of our faith, or will we stumble over Him, rejecting the salvation He offers? As Paul declares, "Whosoever believeth on Him shall not be ashamed" (Romans 10:11). The choice is ours to make: to trust in Christ as our sanctuary or to stumble over Him as our offense.

CHAPTER 13

---

## THE MESSIAH

*The Messiah: The Mighty God — A Study of Isaiah 9:6 and John 4:25-26*

The identity of Jesus Christ as the Messiah is one of the central claims of the New Testament, affirming His divine nature and mission as the Savior of the world. In Isaiah 9:6, the prophet foretells the coming of a child who would be called "Wonderful Counselor, Mighty God, Everlasting Father, Prince of Peace." The title "Mighty God" (Hebrew: El Gibbor) emphasizes not only the Messiah's authority but also His divine identity. This is an unmistakable declaration of the Messiah as more than just a human figure—He is God incarnate.

In John 4:25-26, when Jesus speaks with the Samaritan woman at the well, He directly claims to be the Messiah:

> "The woman saith unto him, I know that Messiah cometh, which is called Christ: when he is come, he will tell us all things. Jesus saith unto her, I that speak unto thee am he." (John 4:25-26, KJV)

By claiming to be the Messiah, Jesus implicitly claimed the titles and attributes ascribed to the Messiah in the Old Testament, including "Mighty God." This chapter will delve into the profound theological meaning of Jesus' messianic identity, how the term "Mighty God" applies to Him, and the significance of His claims in light of the expectations of Israel. Using Strong's Concordance, we will also break down the original Hebrew and Greek terms to gain a deeper understanding of the divine nature of the Messiah.

The Prophecy of Isaiah: The Mighty God

Isaiah 9:6 is one of the most famous and theologically rich Messianic prophecies in the Old Testament. It reads:

> "For unto us a child is born, unto us a son is given: and the government shall be upon His shoulder: and His name shall be called Wonderful, Counselor, The Mighty God, The Everlasting Father, The Prince of Peace." (Isaiah 9:6, KJV)

This passage outlines a series of exalted titles for the promised Messiah, and among them is the title "Mighty God." The term used here is "El Gibbor" in Hebrew, which literally means "God the Warrior" or "God the Mighty One." The word El (H410 in Strong's Concordance) is the common Hebrew word for God, used throughout the Old Testament to refer to the divine. The word Gibbor (H1368 in Strong's Concordance) means mighty, strong, or valiant and is often associated with warriors or powerful leaders.

Key Terms from Strong's Concordance:

- El (H410, אֵל): God, the mighty one. This is a title used exclusively for deity in the Old Testament, indicating the divine nature of the Messiah.

- Gibbor (H1368, גִּבּוֹר): Mighty, strong, valiant, referring to strength and power, often used in a military or leadership context.

The title "Mighty God" indicates that the child to be born would not only rule over Israel but would possess divine power and authority. The Messiah would be more than a human king; He would be God incarnate, capable of delivering His people with divine strength.

Jesus' Claim to be the Messiah: John 4:25-26

In John 4, Jesus meets a Samaritan woman at a well, where He initiates a conversation about living water, worship, and the nature of God. As their dialogue progresses, the woman reveals her understanding of the coming Messiah:

> "The woman saith unto him, I know that Messiah cometh, which is called Christ: when he is come, he will tell us all things." (John 4:25, KJV)

This statement reflects a common Jewish (and even Samaritan) expectation that the Messiah would be a divinely sent figure who would reveal the fullness of God's truth and deliver His people. In response to the woman's statement, Jesus makes one of His clearest declarations of His identity:

> "Jesus saith unto her, I that speak unto thee am he." (John 4:26, KJV)

By claiming to be the Messiah, Jesus is claiming all of the prophetic titles and attributes given to the Messiah in the Old Testament, including the title "Mighty God" from Isaiah 9:6. This is a profound assertion of His divine nature and mission, as the Jews would have understood the Messiah to be the one sent by God to establish His kingdom.

Key Terms from Strong's Concordance:

- Messiah (G3323, Μεσσίας): The anointed one, the Christ. This term refers to the promised deliverer and king of Israel, who would be sent by God to establish His reign.

- Christ (G5547, Χριστός): The Greek equivalent of the Hebrew word Messiah, meaning anointed one. In the New Testament, Christ is the title used to refer to Jesus as the fulfillment of the Old Testament messianic prophecies.

Jesus' claim to be the Messiah is not just a claim to be a human prophet or leader; it is a claim to be God's chosen deliverer, endowed with divine authority, and to be the Mighty God spoken of in Isaiah 9:6. The Samaritan woman understood that the Messiah would reveal all truth, but Jesus revealed much more: that the Messiah Himself is God in human form.

Messianic Expectations and the Divinity of Christ

For the Jews of the first century, the Messiah was expected to be a kingly figure, a descendant of David who would restore Israel's political and spiritual fortunes. However, the full divine identity of the Messiah, as prophesied in Isaiah 9:6, was not widely recognized. Many Jewish leaders and teachers expected the Messiah to be a powerful human king, but they failed to grasp the full implications of prophecies like Isaiah 9:6, which declared the Messiah to be Mighty God.

The New Testament writers, however, clearly saw Jesus as the fulfillment of Isaiah's prophecy. By applying the title Mighty God to Jesus, the apostles and early Christians affirmed His divine nature and His equality with God the Father. This is especially clear in passages like John 1:1:

> "In the beginning was the Word, and the Word was with God, and the Word was God." (John 1:1, KJV)

John's Gospel, in particular, emphasizes that Jesus is not merely a human messiah but the eternal Word of God, fully divine and fully human. The title Mighty God fits perfectly with this portrayal of Jesus as the incarnate deity.

Theological Implications: Jesus as Mighty God

The declaration of Jesus as Mighty God has profound theological implications for our understanding of His nature and mission. As Mighty God, Jesus is more than a teacher, prophet, or political leader—He is the incarnation of the divine, the very power of God in human form. This understanding elevates the significance of His life, death, and resurrection, showing that it is through His divine power that He conquers sin and death and establishes His eternal kingdom.

Jesus as the Divine Warrior:

The term Gibbor (Mighty) often carries the connotation of a warrior or conqueror. In this sense, Jesus is the divine warrior who fights on behalf of His people, defeating the forces of sin, death, and Satan. This theme is echoed in the New Testament, where Jesus is portrayed as the victorious king who will return to judge the world and establish His kingdom (Revelation 19:11-16).

Jesus as the Eternal King:

The prophecy of Isaiah 9:6 also speaks of the government being upon His shoulders, indicating that the Messiah would reign as king. As the Mighty God, Jesus' reign is not limited to Israel or to the first century—it is an eternal reign that encompasses all creation. In Revelation 11:15, we see the culmination of this reign:

> "The kingdoms of this world are become the kingdoms of our Lord, and of His Christ; and He shall reign for ever and ever." (Revelation 11:15, KJV)

The Mighty God in Christ

The identity of Jesus Christ as the Mighty God is foundational to Christian theology and underpins the New Testament's portrayal of His divinity, mission, and redemptive work. When Isaiah prophesied that the coming Messiah would be called El Gibbor — the Mighty God — it was a direct reference to the Messiah's divine nature, affirming that He would be both human and divine. This title, echoed in various ways throughout the Scriptures, highlights Christ's divine authority, power, and eternal nature.

In the New Testament, Jesus fulfilled the prophecies of Isaiah by demonstrating His divine attributes. In John 4:25-26, when He claimed to be the Messiah, He was implicitly claiming all the titles given to the Messiah, including Mighty God. As God incarnate, Jesus did more than fulfill Jewish expectations of a political ruler; He manifested the very power of God on earth through His miracles, teachings, and, ultimately, His death and resurrection. He was Emmanuel—"God with us" (Matt. 1:23)—walking among humanity to offer salvation.

The New Testament writers consistently affirm Jesus' divinity, particularly through their application of Old Testament titles and prophecies to Him. Paul, John, and other apostles wrote extensively about Christ's divine nature. For example, in John 1:1, Jesus is presented as the eternal Word, both with God and being God from the beginning. Paul similarly teaches in Colossians 2:9 that "in Him dwelleth all the fulness of the Godhead bodily," directly identifying Christ with God's divine essence.

Christ as El Gibbor – The Warrior God

The term El Gibbor carries the imagery of a warrior God, one who defends and delivers His people. Jesus demonstrated this warrior-like quality by conquering sin, death, and Satan through His crucifixion and resurrection. His power is not limited to earthly battles but extends to the spiritual realm, where He fought and triumphed over the powers of darkness. This is further seen in passages like

Revelation 19:11-16, where Christ is depicted as the victorious, divine warrior returning in glory.

Jesus' divine power was also manifest in His authority over nature, sickness, demonic forces, and even death itself. His ability to command the winds and waves (Mark 4:39), heal the sick (Mark 1:40-42), and raise the dead (John 11:43-44) are demonstrations of His divine might—something only El Gibbor, the Mighty God, could accomplish.

The Significance of Jesus as the Mighty God

Understanding Jesus as the Mighty God is not just a theological truth to be acknowledged but a reality that has profound implications for Christian faith and life. As the Mighty God, Jesus is able to:

- Save Completely: Because He is God, His sacrifice on the cross has infinite value, fully satisfying the requirements of divine justice and offering complete redemption for those who believe.

- Intercede Eternally: As both human and divine, Jesus intercedes for believers at the right hand of the Father (Hebrews 7:25). His role as our advocate is grounded in His eternal and divine nature.

- Reign Supremely: Jesus' authority as Mighty God ensures that He reigns supreme over all creation. His victory is complete, and His kingdom is eternal (Revelation 11:15).

In the same way that Isaiah 9:6 foretold the Messiah's titles as Wonderful Counselor and Prince of Peace, so too does His title of Mighty God assure believers that Jesus is their ultimate source of strength, protection, and salvation. He is not a distant or powerless deity, but the Almighty God who is actively involved in the redemption and preservation of His people.

Final Thoughts: Worshiping the Mighty God

As Christians, recognizing Jesus as the Mighty God should lead to deep worship, reverence, and submission. Just as Isaiah envisioned a future king who would bring peace and justice through divine strength, we now look back at the incarnation of Jesus and forward to His second coming with great anticipation. Understanding His divinity enriches our faith, as we realize that the same Mighty God who laid the foundations of the earth (Hebrews 1:10-12) is the one who sustains us and has secured our eternal future.

Ultimately, when we declare that Jesus is the Mighty God, we are affirming the profound truth that He is not merely a good teacher or an enlightened prophet, but the very

God who created, redeems, and sustains the universe. This reality transforms how we view His work in history, His role in our lives, and His authority over all things. Through Him, we see the perfect revelation of God's power and love, embodied in the person of Christ.

As believers, our response to this revelation should be one of awe, devotion, and gratitude, for the Mighty God has come near to us in the person of Jesus Christ—Emmanuel, God with us.

# CHAPTER 14

# JOHN THE BAPTIST PREPARING THE WAY FOR YHWH AND THE INDENTITY OF JESUS AS LORD

The identity of Jesus Christ as YHWH (the covenant name of God) is a profound truth that emerges through the ministry of John the Baptist, the forerunner of Christ. In the Old Testament, it was foretold that a messenger would come to prepare the way for YHWH (Isaiah 40:3). In the New Testament, the gospel writers confirm that this prophecy was fulfilled by John the Baptist, who prepared the way for Jesus Christ. Therefore, the direct implication is that Jesus is YHWH, God incarnate.

The Prophecy of Isaiah 40:3 and Its Fulfillment in Christ

In Isaiah 40:3, the prophet speaks of a voice crying out in the wilderness: "Prepare ye the way of the Lord, make straight in the desert a highway for our God." This prophetic voice is preparing the way for YHWH, the God of Israel. The significance of this passage is rooted in the divine identity of the one for whom the way is being prepared. YHWH, the covenant God of Israel, was coming to visit His people.

In the New Testament, Matthew 3:3 applies this passage directly to John the Baptist: "For this is he that was spoken of by the prophet Esaias, saying, The voice of one crying in the wilderness, Prepare ye the way of the Lord, make his paths straight." By attributing this passage to John, the gospel writers make a clear statement: the Lord for whom John is preparing the way is Jesus. Therefore, the conclusion is inescapable—Jesus is YHWH.

This connection is further established when John himself declares that he is not the Messiah but the one sent to prepare the way for the coming of the Lord. In John 1:23, John identifies himself with Isaiah's prophecy: "I am the voice of one crying in the wilderness, Make straight the way of the Lord, as said the prophet Esaias." John's ministry was entirely centered on preparing Israel for the arrival of their God, who, as revealed, was none other than Jesus Christ.

John's Baptism and Jesus' Command for Baptism

John's mission of preparing the way for Christ was directly tied to his practice of baptism. He called people to repentance, and the act of baptism was a sign of their preparation for the coming Messiah. John 1:29-31 tells us that

John baptized to reveal Jesus to Israel: "Behold the Lamb of God, which taketh away the sin of the world… that he should be made manifest to Israel, therefore am I come baptizing with water." John's baptism was a preparatory sign, pointing to the greater work of redemption that Christ would accomplish.

Later, Christ Himself would command the practice of baptism as a necessary part of salvation and the remission of sins. In Mark 16:16, Jesus declares: "He that believeth and is baptized shall be saved; but he that believeth not shall be damned." Baptism, which John had used to prepare people for the coming of Christ, was now a direct command from Christ, linked to the reception of salvation. This is further emphasized in Acts 2:38, where Peter echoes Christ's teaching: "Repent, and be baptized every one of you in the name of Jesus Christ for the remission of sins."

John the Baptist's Role and the Divinity of Christ

The Gospel of Luke adds an important detail to our understanding of John's role in preparing the way for Jesus. In Luke 1:16-17, the angel Gabriel speaks to Zechariah, John's father, and prophesies about John's future ministry: "And many of the children of Israel shall he turn to the Lord their God. And he shall go before him in the spirit and power of Elias, to turn the hearts of the fathers to the children, and the disobedient to the wisdom of the just; to make ready a people prepared for the Lord."

This passage is particularly significant because it describes John as going before the Lord their God. The one for whom John prepares the way is explicitly called "the Lord their God," which in the context of the Old Testament would be understood as YHWH. Therefore, when John goes before Jesus, this passage implies that Jesus is indeed the Lord their God—YHWH incarnate.

This is further confirmed in John 20:28, where Thomas addresses the risen Christ as "My Lord and my God." This exclamation is not merely a statement of reverence but a recognition of Jesus' divine identity. Thomas acknowledges Jesus as both Lord and God, affirming the truth that Jesus is YHWH.

The Stumbling Block to the Jews

The Jews of Jesus' time understood the implications of His claims to divinity, which is why they sought to kill Him. John 5:18 tells us, "Therefore the Jews sought the more to kill him, because he not only had broken the sabbath, but said also that God was his Father, making himself equal with God." The Jews recognized that Jesus was claiming equality with God, which to them was blasphemy—unless, of course, it was true.

This stumbling block is echoed in Romans 9:33, where Paul writes: "As it is written, Behold, I lay in Zion a stumbling stone and rock of offence: and whosoever believeth on him shall not be ashamed." Paul, quoting from Isaiah 8:14, applies the title of the stumbling stone to Jesus, thereby identifying Him with YHWH, who was called the rock of offense in the Old Testament.

Jesus is YHWH, the Covenant God of Israel

The role of John the Baptist in preparing the way for Jesus is clear evidence of Jesus' divine identity as YHWH. The Old Testament prophecies about YHWH coming to His people are fulfilled in the person of Jesus Christ. John's ministry, his baptism, and his witness all pointed to Jesus as the Lord their God—the I AM who appeared to Moses in the burning bush (Exodus 3:14), the rock of offense (Isaiah 8:13-14), and the Mighty God (Isaiah 9:6).

Through John's testimony, the early Christians came to understand that the one who walked among them, performed miracles, and gave His life for the sins of the world was none other than YHWH Himself, in the flesh. This truth is at the heart of the Christian faith: Jesus is Lord, and as Lord, He is YHWH—God with us, the Savior of the world, and the one who holds all authority in heaven and earth (Matthew 28:18).

Believers are therefore called to recognize Jesus not merely as a great teacher or prophet but as the eternal God who has come to save His people. Just as John prepared the way for YHWH, so too must we prepare our hearts to receive and worship Jesus as Lord and God.

CHAPTER 15

# JESUS AS "THE FIRST AND THE LAST"

*Jesus as "The First and the Last" – The Eternal Nature of Christ and His Identity as YHWH*

Throughout the Scriptures, both Old Testament and New Testament, the phrase "the First and the Last" is used as a title of YHWH (God) and is also applied directly to Jesus Christ. This phrase, laden with meaning, emphasizes the eternal, self-existent nature of God. In the Old Testament, it is used to describe the uniqueness and sovereignty of YHWH over all creation, history, and time. In the New Testament, Jesus explicitly claims this title for Himself, revealing His divine identity and eternal existence. The connection between these two uses of the title establishes that Jesus is YHWH.

YHWH: The First and the Last in Isaiah

The title "the First and the Last" appears multiple times in the Book of Isaiah to describe YHWH as the eternal, unchanging, and sovereign God. These passages highlight that there is none before God and none after Him; He is the beginning and the end of all things.

In Isaiah 41:4, God declares, "Who hath wrought and done it, calling the generations from the beginning? I the LORD, the first, and with the last; I am He." Here, YHWH establishes His identity as the eternal God who exists before all creation and who will remain after all things. He is not only the Creator but also the Sustainer of time itself.

Similarly, in Isaiah 44:6, God again uses this title: "Thus saith the LORD the King of Israel, and his redeemer the LORD of hosts; I am the first, and I am the last; and beside me there is no God." This verse emphasizes God's absolute uniqueness—there is no other god, no other being who can claim the title "the First and the Last." This is a clear statement of monotheism and the singularity of God's nature.

Finally, in Isaiah 48:12, God reiterates this identity: "Hearken unto me, O Jacob and Israel, my called; I am he; I am the first, I also am the last." In these passages, YHWH is stressing His eternal nature, His unchanging sovereignty, and His exclusivity as the one true God. The use of "the First and the Last" in Isaiah is a clear proclamation of YHWH's divine and eternal nature, a title that is exclusive to Him.

Jesus: The First and the Last in Revelation

In the New Testament, particularly in the Book of Revelation, Jesus Christ explicitly claims the title "the First and the Last" multiple times, making a direct connection to the YHWH of the Old Testament. These declarations by Jesus affirm His divine identity and His role in the eternal plan of God.

In Revelation 1:11, Jesus speaks to the apostle John, saying, "I am Alpha and Omega, the first and the last." The phrase Alpha and Omega is the Greek equivalent of saying "the first and the last," referring to the beginning and the end of all things. Alpha is the first letter of the Greek alphabet, and Omega is the last. By claiming to be both, Jesus is declaring His presence and authority over the entire scope of history and time, from creation to eternity. This is not a title that could belong to a mere prophet or created being; it belongs to God alone.

Again, in Revelation 1:17-18, Jesus says: "Fear not; I am the first and the last: I am he that liveth, and was dead; and, behold, I am alive for evermore, Amen; and have the keys of hell and of death." Here, Jesus not only claims the title of the First and the Last, but also ties it to His victory over death. This is a crucial revelation—the eternal God (the First and the Last) took on human flesh, died, and rose again. This passage affirms the dual nature of Christ as both fully divine and fully human, and it reveals the immortality of Jesus as God incarnate.

Further, in Revelation 2:8, when addressing the church in Smyrna, Jesus says: "These things saith the first and the last, which was dead, and is alive." Once again, Christ connects His eternal nature to His redemptive work. The One who was dead and is now alive is none other than the First and the Last, showing that the same God who created the world has entered into human history, died for sin, and conquered death.

Finally, in Revelation 22:12-13, Jesus proclaims: "And, behold, I come quickly; and my reward is with me, to give every man according as his work shall be. I am Alpha and Omega, the beginning and the end, the first and the last." In this climactic statement, Jesus emphasizes His return as Judge and King, declaring once more that He is the eternal God who encompasses all of history. The phrase "the First and the Last" here underscores His timeless existence and supreme authority over all creation.

The Unity of YHWH and Jesus as the First and the Last

The use of "the First and the Last" in both the Old Testament and the New Testament clearly demonstrates that Jesus Christ is YHWH. In Isaiah, YHWH alone bears this title, showing His eternal sovereignty and divine nature. In

Revelation, Jesus takes on this same title, revealing that He is the same eternal God who was present at creation and who will bring all things to their fulfillment.

This truth is further confirmed in the prologue of the Gospel of John. John 1:1 declares, "In the beginning was the Word, and the Word was with God, and the Word was God." Jesus is identified as the eternal Word, who was not only with God but was also God Himself. John 1:14 reveals that this eternal Word "was made flesh, and dwelt among us," identifying Jesus as the incarnate YHWH. The First and the Last, who created all things, entered into human history to bring salvation to His people.

The apostle Paul echoes this truth in Colossians 1:16-17, where he writes of Christ: "For by him were all things created, that are in heaven, and that are in earth, visible and invisible... and he is before all things, and by him all things consist." Jesus is described as the preexistent Creator, the One who holds all things together, further confirming His identity as the First and the Last.

Strong's Concordance Analysis

- First (Strong's G4413, protos): This Greek word means "the first in time or place, the foremost, chief, or principal." When Jesus uses this term, He is claiming to be the origin of all things, the preeminent One who stands before all creation.

- Last (Strong's G2078, eschatos): This word signifies "the last in time or place, the final, or ultimate." Jesus is not only the beginning but also the end—the One who will bring all things to their ultimate fulfillment.

Conclusion: Jesus, the Eternal God

The title "the First and the Last" reveals the eternal nature of both YHWH in the Old Testament and Jesus in the New Testament. Through this title, we understand that Jesus is God, eternally existent, and sovereign over all time and space. This is not a title that could be applied to anyone other than God Himself. Jesus' claim to be the First and the Last is a direct assertion of His divinity and His role as the eternal Creator and Sustainer of all things.

The recognition of Jesus as the First and the Last calls for a response of worship, awe, and reverence. As the Alpha and Omega, He is the One who holds the keys to life and death, the One who will come again in glory to judge the living and the dead. Believers are called to trust in His eternal sovereignty, knowing that He is the beginning and the end, and that in Him, all things find their meaning and purpose.

This revelation of Jesus as the First and the Last is a central truth of the Christian faith. It establishes that Jesus is not merely a historical figure or a moral teacher but the eternal God who reigns over all creation. As we recognize Jesus as YHWH, we are called to submit to His lordship and place our faith in Him as the One who was, who is, and who is to come—the First and the Last.

# CHAPTER 16

## THE GLORY OF YHWH AND THE SHARED GLORY OF THE SON

The concept of glory is central in Scripture to the identity of YHWH (God) and His relationship with humanity. In Isaiah 42:8, God declares emphatically, "I am the LORD [YHWH]: that is my name: and my glory will I not give to another, neither my praise to graven images." This statement speaks to the unique and incomparable nature of God's glory. However, in the New Testament, we see that this glory is indeed shared, but only between the Father and the Son, Jesus Christ. In multiple passages, Jesus is revealed as sharing in the divine glory of YHWH, affirming His divine status and His unity with the Father. This chapter explores the theological implications of shared glory within the Godhead, focusing on key passages and an analysis of the Strong's Concordance to provide a comprehensive understanding.

YHWH's Exclusive Glory in Isaiah 42:8

Isaiah 42:8 presents a fundamental truth about the character of God. The Hebrew word used for glory is כָּבוֹד (kabod) [Strong's H3519], which means weight, honor, or splendor. God's glory refers to the manifestation of His presence, power, and holiness. It is intrinsic to His being, and in this passage, YHWH makes it clear that His glory cannot be shared with any other being, especially idols or false gods.

This declaration is important because it asserts that YHWH alone is worthy of worship and adoration. His glory is a reflection of His sovereignty, holiness, and supreme power. The refusal to share His glory reinforces the fact that God is unique in His divine essence. This becomes particularly significant when we later examine how Jesus participates in this very glory.

Jesus' Prayer for Glory in John 17:1, 5

In the Gospel of John, Jesus prays to the Father, making a profound request concerning the glory that they share. In John 17:1, Jesus prays, "Father, the hour is come; glorify thy Son, that thy Son also may glorify thee." Here, Jesus acknowledges that the Father's glory is also His own glory and that through His upcoming death and resurrection, this shared glory will be revealed to the world. This prayer demonstrates the inseparable relationship between Father and Son, in which the glory of one glorifies the other.

The most striking statement comes in John 17:5, where Jesus says, "And now, O Father, glorify thou me with thine own self with the glory which I had with thee before the world was." In this verse, Jesus makes a direct claim to eternality and pre-existence with the Father. He speaks of a glory that He shared with the Father before creation, which directly parallels the glory of YHWH described in Isaiah 42:8. This reveals that Jesus was not merely a man or a created being, but He participated in the eternal glory of God Himself.

Jesus as the Radiance of God's Glory (Hebrews 1:3)

The Epistle to the Hebrews further clarifies the relationship between Jesus and the glory of YHWH. In Hebrews 1:3, the writer says of Jesus: "Who being the brightness of his glory, and the express image of his person, and upholding all things by the word of his power, when he had by himself purged our sins, sat down on the right hand of the Majesty on high."

The phrase brightness of His glory is a translation of the Greek word ἀπαύγασμα (apaugasma) [Strong's G541], which means radiance or reflected brightness. This description portrays Jesus as the visible manifestation of God's glory. Just as the brightness of the sun is inseparable from the sun itself, so too is the glory of Jesus inseparable from the glory of God. Jesus is the perfect reflection and representation of the Father's divine glory, and through Him, humanity can perceive the fullness of God's glory.

This verse also emphasizes that Jesus is the exact representation (Greek: χαρακτήρ, charaktēr, Strong's G5481) of God's being. The term charaktēr refers to an engraving or impression, meaning that Jesus perfectly reflects the essence of God. Therefore, when we speak of Jesus sharing the glory of the Father, it is because He is the exact imprint of the divine nature.

The Glory of Christ in Revelation 5:12

The final apocalyptic vision of Christ in the Book of Revelation paints a picture of Jesus sharing in the glory of God and being worshipped as God. In Revelation 5:12, the heavenly beings declare: "Worthy is the Lamb that was slain to receive power, and riches, and wisdom, and strength, and honor, and glory, and blessing." Here, Jesus is identified as the Lamb, a reference to His sacrificial death for sin, and He is given honor and glory—attributes that are typically reserved for YHWH.

The glory given to Jesus here is the same divine glory that YHWH declares He will not share with another in Isaiah 42:8. Yet, in this scene of heavenly worship, Jesus receives glory alongside God the Father. This underscores the deity of Christ and His equality with the Father in divine glory. Revelation 5 is a powerful vision of Jesus' exaltation and the recognition of His divine authority.

Strong's Concordance Analysis

1. Glory (Strong's H3519, kabod): In Isaiah 42:8, the Hebrew word kabod means weightiness, honor, or splendor. It refers to the manifestation of God's presence and is often linked with God's holiness and majesty.

2. Glory (Strong's G1391, doxa): The Greek equivalent of kabod is doxa, which appears in the New Testament and conveys honor, praise, and majesty. In John 17:1, 5, doxa is used to describe the shared glory between Jesus and the Father.

3. Radiance (Strong's G541, apaugasma): In Hebrews 1:3, this term is used to describe Jesus as the radiance or brightness of God's glory, meaning He is the visible expression of the Father's divine essence.

4. Image (Strong's G5481, charaktēr): This word refers to an engraving or impression and is used to describe Jesus as the exact representation of God's nature in Hebrews 1:3.

The glory that YHWH declares He will not share with another in Isaiah 42:8 is uniquely shared with Jesus Christ, demonstrating the profound truth that Jesus is divine and one with the Father. As seen in John 17, Hebrews 1, and Revelation 5, Jesus possesses the glory that belongs to YHWH alone, establishing His eternal nature and unity with the Father. This shared glory is not a contradiction of Isaiah 42:8, but a confirmation of the Trinitarian relationship between the Father and Son—two distinct persons sharing the same divine essence and glory. Jesus, as the radiance of God's glory, is the visible manifestation of the invisible God, and through Him, we behold the fullness of God's glory.

CHAPTER 17

---

# THE UNIVERSAL LORDSHIP OF JESUS

*The Universal Lordship of Jesus (YHWH) and the Submission of Every Knee*

Throughout the Bible, YHWH is depicted as the sole Sovereign to whom all creation must eventually submit. In Isaiah 45:21-23, YHWH proclaims His supremacy over all, stating that every knee will bow to Him, a declaration of His divine right to absolute worship and recognition. The Apostle Paul, in his letters to the Romans and the Philippians, attributes this same universal submission to Jesus Christ. This parallel establishes that the Lord Jesus is not merely a figure of human authority, but He shares the same divine sovereignty as YHWH, affirming His identity as God.

This chapter will explore these passages and their profound theological implications for understanding Christ's deity, His role in Judgment, and His eschatological reign, drawing insights from Strong's Concordance to clarify key terms and provide a more detailed expository study.

YHWH's Declaration of Sovereignty in Isaiah 45:21-23

In Isaiah 45, the prophet speaks on behalf of YHWH, declaring His absolute rule and supremacy over all the earth. Isaiah 45:21-22 reads, "And there is no other god besides me, a righteous God and a Savior; there is none except me. Turn to me and be saved, all the ends of the earth! For I am God, and there is no other." Here, YHWH asserts that He alone is the Savior and the only God capable of delivering humanity from destruction.

In Isaiah 45:23, YHWH says, "By myself I have sworn, from my mouth has gone out in righteousness a word that shall not return: 'To me every knee shall bow, every tongue shall swear allegiance.'" This powerful proclamation reveals the inexorable authority of God, underscoring that in the end, every created being—both those who serve Him and those who rebel—will be compelled to submit to His sovereignty.

The phrase "every knee shall bow" (Hebrew: כָּל־בֶּרֶךְ תִּכְרַע, Strong's H3766, kara), refers to an act of submission and reverence. It is often used to denote the physical posture of bowing before a king or deity. In the context of YHWH's sovereignty, it is an expression of universal submission to

God's authority, implying that all creatures, even the defiant, must ultimately acknowledge His supremacy.

The Application to Jesus in Romans 14:10-11 and Philippians 2:10-11

The Apostle Paul takes the imagery from Isaiah 45:23 and applies it directly to Jesus Christ in his writings. In Romans 14:10-11, Paul echoes the words of Isaiah: "For we shall all stand before the judgment seat of Christ. For it is written, 'As I live, says the Lord, every knee shall bow to me, and every tongue shall confess to God.'" Paul here draws a direct connection between Christ and YHWH, indicating that Jesus, in His role as Judge, will receive the same submission and worship that YHWH claims for Himself in Isaiah 45.

In Philippians 2:10-11, Paul further amplifies this theme by stating that at the name of Jesus, "every knee should bow, of things in heaven, and things in earth, and things under the earth; And that every tongue should confess that Jesus Christ is Lord, to the glory of God the Father." The phrase "Jesus Christ is Lord" (Greek: Κύριος Ἰησοῦς Χριστός, Strong's G2962, kyrios) directly attributes the title of Lord to Jesus, a title that in both the Greek Septuagint (LXX) and the New Testament is frequently used for YHWH. This underscores Jesus' divine status as the one to whom all creation owes ultimate allegiance.

Jesus as Judge and the Revelation of His Glory

Another essential element in the New Testament depiction of Jesus is His role as the divine Judge who will preside over the final judgment. Several passages, such as Matthew 25:31-33 and 2 Thessalonians 1:7-9, affirm that Jesus will appear at the end of time to judge the nations. This is in harmony with the Old Testament teaching that YHWH is the Judge of the whole earth (Psalm 96:13; Isaiah 33:22).

In Matthew 25:31-32, Jesus describes the scene of Judgment Day: "When the Son of Man comes in his glory, and all the angels with him, then he will sit on his glorious throne. Before him will be gathered all the nations, and he will separate people one from another as a shepherd separates the sheep from the goats." Here, Jesus refers to Himself as the Son of Man who will come in glory (Greek: δόξα, doxa, Strong's G1391), a term associated with divine splendor and often used in the Septuagint to describe YHWH's glory. Jesus sits on the throne of judgment, where He determines the eternal fate of humanity, underscoring His absolute authority.

Furthermore, Philippians 2:10-11 reveals that this act of universal submission to Jesus serves to glorify the Father. The shared glory between Father and Son becomes evident as

Jesus' exaltation is tied to the Father's divine purpose, fulfilling the prophecy in Isaiah that every knee would bow to YHWH.

The Wicked Will Kneel Before Jesus on Judgment Day

One of the most sobering aspects of Judgment Day is that even the wicked, those who have rejected God, will be forced to kneel before Jesus. According to Matthew 25:31-46, when Jesus returns, He will separate the righteous from the wicked, rewarding the former with eternal life and condemning the latter to eternal punishment. Titus 2:13 also describes this event, referring to the return of Christ as the blessed hope for believers, but it also signifies the day of reckoning for those who remain in rebellion.

Although Matthew 5:8 and Hebrews 12:14 suggest that only the pure in heart and those who strive for holiness will see God in His full glory, everyone—including the wicked—will see Jesus when He comes to judge. In 1 Thessalonians 4:16-17 and 2 Thessalonians 1:7-9, Paul describes the glorious appearance of Jesus at His second coming, when all will be gathered before Him. Even those who have rejected Him will be unable to escape His divine presence, and they too will be forced to bow in recognition of His authority.

Strong's Concordance Analysis

1. Knee (Strong's H3766, kara'): The Hebrew term kara' means to bend the knee in submission or reverence. In Isaiah 45:23, the bending of the knee symbolizes complete submission to YHWH's authority.

2. Bow (Strong's G2578, kamptō): In the New Testament, the Greek word kamptō is used to describe bowing in submission. In Philippians 2:10, it refers to the act of kneeling before Jesus, signifying that all beings will ultimately acknowledge His lordship.

3. Lord (Strong's G2962, kyrios): This Greek term means lord, master, or owner. In Philippians 2:11, Jesus is confessed as Lord, emphasizing His divine sovereignty and equality with YHWH.

4. Confess (Strong's G1843, exomologeō): The Greek word exomologeō means to acknowledge or declare openly. In Philippians 2:11, it refers to the universal confession that Jesus is Lord, affirming His divine authority.

The universal submission of all creation to Jesus Christ on the Day of Judgment affirms His divine identity as YHWH. Just as YHWH declared in Isaiah 45:23 that every knee would bow and every tongue would confess to Him, the

Apostle Paul explicitly applies this to Jesus in both Romans 14:10-11 and Philippians 2:10-11. This profound truth reinforces that Jesus, who shares the glory and authority of the Father, is indeed God. His sovereignty is not merely temporal or limited to the earthly realm but extends to the cosmic order, as all things in heaven, on earth, and under the earth will bow before Him.

In addition, the eschatological expectation that all will see and submit to Jesus highlights His role as the divine Judge. Although the wicked will not see the Father in His full glory, they will bow before Jesus, acknowledging His authority, even as they face eternal separation from Him. Matthew 25:31-33, 1 Thessalonians 4:16-17, and 2 Thessalonians 1:7-9 describe this climactic moment when Christ returns in glory, fulfilling His role as Judge and Savior.

Furthermore, the New Testament repeatedly identifies Jesus with titles and descriptions reserved for YHWH in the Old Testament. He is the first and the last (Isaiah 41:4; Revelation 1:17), the Rock of offense (Isaiah 8:13-14; Romans 9:33), and the Mighty God (Isaiah 9:6). His identity as Immanuel, meaning "God with us" (Isaiah 7:14; Matthew 1:23), encapsulates the heart of the Christian faith: that God

Himself came to dwell among humanity in the person of Jesus Christ.

Ultimately, the biblical testimony—supported by the Strong's Concordance and other theological tools—points to the reality that Jesus Christ is not a mere prophet, teacher, or moral guide. He is the eternal Son of God, sharing the very essence of the Father. As such, He is worthy of the same worship and submission that belongs to YHWH alone. On the last day, when every knee bows and every tongue confesses that Jesus is Lord, it will be the final and ultimate acknowledgment of His deity and sovereignty over all creation.

CHAPTER 18

---

# THE FUFLLMENT OF JOEL'S PROPHECY IN CHRIST

*The Fulfillment of Joel's Prophecy in Christ — Calling on the Name of YHWH for Salvation*

In Joel 2:32, the prophet declares, "And it shall come to pass, that whosoever shall call on the name of YHWH shall be delivered." This verse encapsulates the promise of salvation for those who turn to YHWH. However, the New Testament writers, particularly in Acts 2:21 and Romans 10:9-13, apply this declaration directly to Jesus Christ, affirming that calling on the name of Jesus is synonymous with calling on YHWH for salvation.

This chapter will provide an expository study and comprehensive commentary on this concept, demonstrating that the New Testament clearly teaches the divine identity of Jesus by applying Joel's prophecy to Him. We will explore the Strong's Concordance for key terms in these passages and analyze the connection between the Old Testament and New Testament references to calling on YHWH and Jesus for salvation.

The Prophecy in Joel (Joel 2:32)

Joel 2:32 states, "And it shall come to pass, that whosoever shall call on the name of the LORD [YHWH] shall be delivered: for in Mount Zion and in Jerusalem shall be deliverance, as the LORD hath said, and in the remnant whom the LORD shall call."

The phrase "call on the name" comes from the Hebrew word קָרָא (qara, Strong's H7121), meaning to call out, cry unto, or invoke. In this context, it denotes invoking YHWH's help in the midst of a dire situation, specifically during the prophesied Day of the Lord. The name of YHWH signifies His authority, character, and power. Thus, to "call on the name of YHWH" is to trust in His sovereignty and rely on His deliverance.

Joel's prophecy refers to a future time of salvation, where YHWH would deliver those who turn to Him. This promise of salvation becomes universal with the inclusion of the Gentiles (non-Jews), indicating that it is not limited to the people of Israel alone. This theme of universal salvation is a key concept that will be expanded upon in the New

Testament, where the promise of deliverance through YHWH is extended to all who call on the name of Jesus.

The Fulfillment in the New Testament

Acts 2:21 and Peter's Sermon

In Acts 2:21, the Apostle Peter quotes Joel 2:32 during his sermon on the Day of Pentecost: "And it shall come to pass, that whosoever shall call on the name of the Lord shall be saved." Here, the Greek word for "call" is ἐπικαλέω (epikaleō, Strong's G1941), which similarly means to call upon or invoke a name for help.

Peter's use of Joel's prophecy in Acts 2 shows that the New Testament writers saw Jesus as the fulfillment of YHWH's promise of deliverance. In the same sermon, Peter emphasizes that Jesus of Nazareth is the Messiah and Lord. He goes on to explain that salvation comes through repentance and baptism in the name of Jesus Christ for the forgiveness of sins (Acts 2:38).

This connection is crucial because it demonstrates that calling on the name of YHWH for salvation is now understood as calling on the name of Jesus. This theological shift is not a contradiction but a fulfillment of Joel's prophecy in the light of the New Covenant, where Jesus is revealed as

YHWH incarnate, the Savior through whom salvation is realized.

Romans 10:9-13 and Paul's Teaching

In Romans 10:9-13, the Apostle Paul makes a profound declaration regarding salvation: "If thou shalt confess with thy mouth the Lord Jesus, and shalt believe in thine heart that God hath raised him from the dead, thou shalt be saved. For with the heart man believeth unto righteousness, and with the mouth confession is made unto salvation. For the scripture saith, Whosoever believeth on him shall not be ashamed... For whosoever shall call upon the name of the Lord shall be saved."

Paul quotes Joel 2:32 in Romans 10:13, affirming that calling on the name of Jesus is the means of salvation. The title "Lord" in this passage is translated from the Greek word κύριος (kyrios, Strong's G2962), which is the equivalent of YHWH in the Septuagint (the Greek translation of the Old Testament). Thus, by calling Jesus "Lord," Paul is equating Him with YHWH.

Paul's teaching emphasizes that salvation is now accessible to all—Jews and Gentiles—through faith in Jesus Christ. The righteousness that comes by faith is not based on works of the law but on believing in the finished work of Christ on the cross and His resurrection.

Theological Implications of Calling on Jesus as YHWH

The application of Joel's prophecy to Jesus has significant theological implications. By stating that calling on the name of Jesus results in salvation, the New Testament writers make an unmistakable assertion of Christ's divinity. Jesus is not merely a representative of YHWH; He is YHWH Himself, the incarnate Word who fulfills the promises of the Old Covenant.

1. Jesus as YHWH: The title "Lord" in the New Testament is a direct reference to the divine name of YHWH in the Old Testament. This means that calling on the name of Jesus is calling on the name of YHWH, further establishing that Jesus is God in the fullest sense.

2. Universal Salvation: Joel's prophecy of deliverance is expanded in the New Testament to include all nations. Paul's declaration that "whosoever shall call upon the name of the Lord shall be saved" (Romans 10:13) reveals the universal scope of God's grace, extending to both Jews and Gentiles through Jesus Christ.

3. The Unity of the Father and Son: Although Jesus and the Father are distinct persons within the Godhead, they share the same divine essence. The Father has given all

authority to the Son (John 3:35), so calling on the name of Jesus is also a recognition of the Father's authority and plan of salvation.

Strong's Concordance Analysis

- Call (ἐπικαλέω, Strong's G1941): To invoke or call upon for aid or salvation.

- Lord (κύριος, Strong's G2962): Used in the New Testament as a direct reference to YHWH, affirming Jesus' divine status.

- Saved (σώζω, Strong's G4982): To be delivered or rescued from sin and eternal death.

In both Acts 2:21 and Romans 10:13, the New Testament applies Joel's prophecy about calling on the name of YHWH to Jesus Christ, showing that the means of salvation in the New Covenant is through calling upon Jesus' name. The apostles clearly affirm that Jesus is the Lord and YHWH prophesied in the Old Testament, and that salvation is available to all who place their faith in Him.

This truth underscores the divine nature of Jesus Christ and His role as the one who fulfills the promises of YHWH in the Old Testament. By calling on the name of Jesus, we call on YHWH for our salvation, affirming that Jesus is the incarnate God and the source of eternal life. The promise of deliverance, once confined to Israel, is now available to all who believe in Jesus Christ, making Him the fulfillment of Joel's prophecy and the hope of the world.

# CHAPTER 19

## THE RIGHTEOUS BRANCH OF DAVID

*The Righteous Branch of David – YHWH Our Righteousness*

In Jeremiah 23:5-6, the prophet foretells the coming of a righteous Branch from the line of David who will reign as King and be known by the divine name YHWH Tsidkenu ("The LORD our righteousness"). This prophecy directly points to Jesus Christ, who, as a descendant of David, is the fulfillment of the promise of a righteous King who would execute justice and bring salvation. This chapter explores the significance of this prophecy, focusing on the identity of Jesus as YHWH, His righteous reign, and the fulfillment of Old Testament prophecies regarding the Messiah. Using Strong's Concordance, we will dissect key terms and their theological implications.

The Prophecy in Jeremiah: The Righteous Branch (Jer. 23:5-6)

Jeremiah's prophecy is one of hope amidst the chaos of Judah's impending destruction. The promise of a righteous

Branch from the line of David provides a messianic vision of restoration and justice:

- Jeremiah 23:5-6: "Behold, the days come, saith the LORD, that I will raise unto David a righteous Branch, and a King shall reign and prosper, and shall execute judgment and justice in the earth. In his days Judah shall be saved, and Israel shall dwell safely: and this is his name whereby he shall be called, THE LORD OUR RIGHTEOUSNESS."

Key Terms:

- Branch (צֶמַח, tsemach, Strong's H6780): A sprout, shoot, or offspring. This term is often used to refer to the Messianic figure emerging from the line of David, symbolizing new life and restoration.

- Righteous (צַדִּיק, tsaddiq, Strong's H6662): Just, lawful, or morally right. The Branch will embody perfect righteousness, in contrast to the unrighteous leaders of Israel at the time of Jeremiah.

- YHWH Tsidkenu (יְהוָה צִדְקֵנוּ, YHWH Tsidkenu, Strong's H3072): "The LORD our righteousness." This name for the Messiah directly identifies Him with YHWH, affirming the divinity of the coming King.

The Branch is not just a future king but is YHWH Himself, coming in human form to bring righteousness and justice to the earth. This association of the Branch with YHWH underscores the fact that the Messiah will not be merely a political figure but a divine ruler.

The Branch of David: Jesus Christ

In the New Testament, the genealogy of Jesus (Matthew 1:1-17; Luke 3:23-38) confirms His lineage as a direct descendant of David, fulfilling the promise of a Davidic King. Jesus' ministry, death, and resurrection demonstrated His role as the righteous ruler who brings salvation to all, both Judah and Israel—a unification of God's people.

- Luke 1:32-33: "He shall be great, and shall be called the Son of the Highest: and the Lord God shall give unto him the throne of his father David: and he shall reign over the house of Jacob forever; and of his kingdom there shall be no end."

Jesus fulfills the role of the Davidic Branch prophesied in Jeremiah 23:5-6, but more significantly, He is identified as YHWH Tsidkenu ("The LORD our righteousness"). His righteousness is not just a quality He possesses but a gift He offers to humanity through faith. In 2 Corinthians 5:21, Paul writes, "For He hath made Him to be sin for us, who knew no sin; that we might be made the righteousness of God in Him." Jesus, the righteous Branch, imparts His righteousness to those who believe in Him.

The Divine Identity of the Branch

Jeremiah's prophecy is unique because it explicitly calls the Messianic figure by the name YHWH. This is a profound statement about the divine identity of the Messiah. Throughout the Old Testament, YHWH is the sole deliverer of His people, and the idea that YHWH Himself would come in the form of the Branch to rule and save is a powerful revelation of the incarnation.

In Zechariah 6:12-13, the prophet reiterates the theme of the Branch: "Thus speaketh the LORD of hosts, saying, Behold the man whose name is The Branch; and he shall grow up out of his place, and he shall build the temple of the LORD: Even he shall build the temple of the LORD; and he shall bear the glory, and shall sit and rule upon his throne; and he shall be a priest upon his throne: and the counsel of peace shall be between them both."

This Branch will build the temple, sit on the throne, and serve as both king and priest, foreshadowing the work of Jesus Christ, who, as the High Priest, offered Himself as the perfect sacrifice and now reigns eternally as King. The role of Jesus as the righteous ruler and the ultimate High Priest further confirms His divine identity and His fulfillment of the Messianic prophecies.

Christ, Our Righteousness

The title YHWH Tsidkenu is crucial to understanding Jesus' role in salvation. The righteousness that Jesus provides is not merely an external judgment of the law; it is the imputed righteousness given to believers through faith in Christ. Paul explains this in detail:

- Romans 3:22-24: "Even the righteousness of God which is by faith of Jesus Christ unto all and upon all them that believe: for there is no difference: For all have sinned, and come short of the glory of God; being justified freely by his grace through the redemption that is in Christ Jesus."

This righteousness is a divine gift that allows believers to stand before God justified and cleansed from sin. Jesus, as YHWH Tsidkenu, fulfills the need for a mediator between God and humanity, providing the perfect righteousness required for salvation. Thus, calling Jesus YHWH Tsidkenu is to acknowledge His divinity and His role as the one who makes us righteous before God.

Strong's Concordance Analysis

- Branch (צֶמַח, tsemach, Strong's H6780): A symbol of new growth and life, representing the Messianic figure from the line of David.

- Righteous (צַדִּיק, tsaddiq, Strong's H6662): Describing the Messiah's character and His role as the one who embodies perfect justice and righteousness.

- YHWH Tsidkenu (יְהוָה צִדְקֵנוּ, YHWH Tsidkenu, Strong's H3072): "The LORD our righteousness." This title emphasizes the divine nature of the Messiah and His role in providing righteousness for believers.

Jesus as YHWH, the Righteous Branch

The Branch of David prophesied in Jeremiah is none other than Jesus Christ, the Messianic King who brings righteousness, justice, and salvation. The title YHWH Tsidkenu—"The LORD our righteousness"—proclaims the divine identity of Christ and His central role in God's plan for the redemption of humanity.

In Christ, we see the fulfillment of the Davidic promise, the embodiment of YHWH's righteousness, and the universal scope of salvation offered to all who believe in His name. The Branch has come, and through His righteousness, we are made right with God. Thus, to call upon Jesus is to call upon YHWH, the one true God, who alone can save and deliver.

CHAPTER 20

---

## JESUS AS ALPHA AND THE OMEGA

*Jesus as the Alpha and the Omega – The Lord God Almighty*

The identification of Jesus as the Alpha and the Omega, the first and the last, and the beginning and the end in the book of Revelation points to His divine nature and eternal sovereignty. In Revelation 1:8, the Lord God Almighty refers to Himself as the Alpha and Omega, a title that represents His eternal existence, while in Revelation 22:13-16, Jesus applies the same title to Himself, further emphasizing His unity with God and His divine authority over all creation. This chapter explores the profound theological implications of these titles, their application to Jesus, and the way they reveal His identity as the Lord God Almighty.

The Alpha and the Omega: An Expression of Divine Eternity

The title Alpha and Omega comes from the first and last letters of the Greek alphabet, symbolizing that God is the beginning and the end of all things. In Revelation 1:8, God declares:

- Revelation 1:8: "I am the Alpha and the Omega, saith the Lord God, who is, who was, and who is to come, the Almighty."

This phrase expresses God's eternality, encompassing past, present, and future. He is the source of all existence and will bring all things to their ultimate conclusion. The term Almighty (παντοκράτωρ, pantokrator, Strong's G3841) further emphasizes His supreme power and authority over all creation.

Key Terms:

- Alpha and Omega (Ἄλφα καὶ τὸ Ὦ, Alpha kai to O, Strong's G1 & G5598): The first and last letters of the Greek alphabet, symbolizing totality and completeness.

- Almighty (παντοκράτωρ, pantokrator, Strong's G3841): One who holds all power, ruler over all things. This title emphasizes God's absolute sovereignty.

The title Alpha and Omega is exclusive to God, denoting His eternal presence and unchanging nature. The same title, however, is later applied directly to Jesus Christ, affirming His deity and role as Lord of all.

Jesus as the Alpha and Omega

In Revelation 22:13, Jesus identifies Himself with the same divine title previously used by God the Father:

- Revelation 22:13-16: "I am the Alpha and the Omega, the first and the last, the beginning and the end… I, Jesus, have sent my angel to testify unto you these things in the churches."

Here, Jesus uses Alpha and Omega to affirm His eternal existence and sovereignty over time and creation, just as YHWH does in Isaiah:

- Isaiah 41:4: "I the Lord, the first, and with the last; I am He."

- Isaiah 44:6: "I am the first, and I am the last; and beside me there is no God."

By identifying Himself as the Alpha and Omega, the first and the last, Jesus is making a clear declaration of His deity. He is the eternal One, co-equal with God the Father, and shares in the same divine identity. The Greek text makes no distinction between the titles used for God and those used for Christ, underscoring the reality that Jesus is fully God.

Key Terms:

- First and Last (πρῶτος καὶ ἔσχατος, protos kai eschatos, Strong's G4413 & G2078): Refers to the one who existed before all things and who will remain after all things, a title of divine eternality.

Jesus as the Almighty

Another significant element in Revelation 1:8 is the term Almighty, which is used to describe God's sovereign rule over the universe. This title is applied to Jesus in other parts of the New Testament, particularly in His post-resurrection glory:

- Revelation 1:17-18: "Fear not; I am the first and the last: I am he that liveth, and was dead; and, behold, I am alive for evermore, Amen; and have the keys of hell and of death."

Here, Jesus affirms His role as the Almighty, emphasizing His authority over life and death. The Greek word for Almighty (pantokrator) is used throughout Revelation to describe the One who holds ultimate power over the cosmos. That same power is ascribed to Jesus, who conquered death and reigns as the eternal King of kings.

Key Terms:

- Keys of Hell and Death (κλεῖς τοῦ ᾅδου καὶ τοῦ θανάτου, kleis tou hadou kai tou thanatou, Strong's G2807, G86, G2288): A symbol of authority over death and the afterlife, signifying Jesus' victory over the grave and His power to give eternal life.

The Unity of Father and Son

The titles Alpha and Omega and Almighty reinforce the oneness of Jesus and the Father. Throughout Revelation, there is a consistent portrayal of Jesus sharing in the glory, authority, and attributes of God the Father. In John 17:5, Jesus prays:

- John 17:5: "And now, O Father, glorify thou me with thine own self with the glory which I had with thee before the world was."

This prayer reflects the pre-existence of Jesus and His eternal glory shared with the Father, which is a clear indication of His divine nature. The Alpha and Omega title, applied both to the Father and to Jesus, shows their unified essence and co-equal authority.

Moreover, the New Testament affirms the divine identity of Jesus by attributing to Him the acts of creation and sustenance of the universe, roles exclusively attributed to YHWH:

- John 1:1-3: "In the beginning was the Word, and the Word was with God, and the Word was God. The same was in the beginning with God. All things were made by Him; and without Him was not anything made that was made."

- Colossians 1:16-17: "For by Him were all things created, that are in heaven, and that are in earth... all things were created by Him, and for Him: And He is before all things, and by Him all things consist."

Strong's Concordance Analysis

- Alpha and Omega (Ἄλφα καὶ τὸ Ὦ, Alpha kai to O, Strong's G1 & G5598): Jesus' claim to be Alpha and Omega emphasizes His eternality and divine nature, being at both the beginning and the end of all things.

- First and Last (πρῶτος καὶ ἔσχατος, protos kai eschatos, Strong's G4413 & G2078): This title confirms Jesus' eternal existence, from the foundation of the world to its consummation.

- Almighty (παντοκράτωρ, pantokrator, Strong's G3841): Jesus as the Almighty reveals His sovereign power over the cosmos, ruling with absolute authority.

- Keys of Hell and Death (κλεῖς τοῦ ᾅδου καὶ τοῦ θανάτου, kleis tou hadou kai tou thanatou, Strong's G2807, G86, G2288): This term shows Jesus' authority over the realms of death, emphasizing His victory through resurrection.

Jesus as Lord God Almighty

The titles Alpha and Omega, First and Last, and Almighty, applied to Jesus in the book of Revelation, are powerful declarations of His divinity. These titles, which are used of God the Father in the Old Testament, are now applied to Jesus, confirming His oneness with YHWH and His eternal rule over all creation.

The New Testament presents Jesus as the Alpha and Omega, the eternal Word of God who was with the Father from the beginning and will reign forever. Through His victory over death and His authority over all creation, Jesus is revealed as the Lord God Almighty, worthy of all honor, worship, and submission.

As believers, acknowledging Jesus as the Alpha and Omega invites us to recognize Him as the center of all existence, from the beginning to the end of time. We worship Him not only as our Savior but also as the Almighty God, who holds the keys to life, death, and eternity.

CHAPTER 21

## THOMAS' CONFESSION AND THE DIVINITY OF CHRIST

In the closing chapters of the Gospel of John, Thomas's confession of faith stands as one of the clearest and most direct affirmations of the divine nature of Jesus Christ. In John 20:28, when Thomas sees the resurrected Christ, he exclaims, "My Lord and my God." This remarkable statement is not rebuked by Jesus; instead, it is accepted as a true and fitting declaration of who Jesus is. The absence of any correction from Jesus in response to Thomas's words underscores the theological significance of this moment. This chapter will explore the implications of Thomas's confession, as well as its connection to the broader Christological themes found throughout Scripture.

Thomas's Confession: "My Lord and My God"

John 20:28 records Thomas's reaction to encountering the risen Christ:

- John 20:28: "Thomas answered and said unto him, My Lord and my God."

In this confession, Thomas directly addresses Jesus as both Lord and God. The Greek words used here—κύριος (kurios, Strong's G2962) for "Lord" and θεός (theos, Strong's G2316) for "God"—are significant. Kurios is often used in the Greek Old Testament (the Septuagint) to translate YHWH, the divine name of God, while theos directly refers to deity. By using both terms, Thomas recognizes not only the resurrection of Jesus but also His full divine nature.

Key Terms:

- Lord (κυριός, kurios, Strong's G2962): A title of honor and authority, frequently used for YHWH in the Old Testament and applied to Jesus in the New Testament.

- God (θεός, theos, Strong's G2316): The title for deity, referring to the one true God in both the Old and New Testaments.

Thomas's confession is a climactic moment in the Gospel of John, as it encapsulates the purpose of the entire book: to show that Jesus is both the Messiah and the Son of God, and that through believing in Him, people may have eternal life (John 20:31).

The Absence of Rebuke: Affirmation of Divinity

One of the most notable aspects of Thomas's declaration is that Jesus does not rebuke him for calling Him God. This contrasts sharply with other instances in the Gospels where Jesus corrects His disciples when they misunderstand or speak out of turn. For instance, in Matthew 16:22-23, when Peter tries to dissuade Jesus from going to the cross, Jesus rebukes him, saying, "Get thee behind me, Satan: thou art an offense unto me: for thou savorest not the things that be of God."

In John 20:28, however, Jesus does not rebuke Thomas. Instead, He responds with affirmation, saying, "Because thou hast seen me, thou hast believed: blessed are they that have not seen, and yet have believed" (John 20:29). The lack of correction implies that what Thomas said was indeed true and "of God." This further solidifies the argument for Jesus's divinity, as Jesus not only accepts worship and divine titles but also encourages belief in His identity as Lord and God.

Theological Implication:

- The absence of rebuke highlights that Thomas's words were not inappropriate or mistaken. If Jesus were not God, this would have been the perfect moment to correct

Thomas. Instead, Jesus blesses Thomas and future believers, implying that this confession is foundational to the Christian faith.

Jesus as Our Divine Lord and God

Throughout the New Testament, Jesus is consistently identified as Lord and God, not only by Thomas but by other apostles and early Christian leaders. For example:

- Romans 9:5: "Of whom as concerning the flesh Christ came, who is over all, God blessed forever."

- Titus 2:13: "Looking for that blessed hope, and the glorious appearing of the great God and our Savior Jesus Christ."

- Hebrews 1:8: "But unto the Son he saith, Thy throne, O God, is for ever and ever."

These verses echo the same divine titles applied to Jesus, affirming His full deity. In the context of Thomas's confession, these verses further strengthen the notion that recognizing Jesus as Lord and God is central to Christian theology.

Key Concepts:

- Jesus as God: Numerous New Testament passages directly refer to Jesus as God, including John 1:1, where the Word (Jesus) is called God, and John 20:28, where Thomas addresses Jesus as God.

- Jesus as Lord: Jesus's lordship is repeatedly affirmed in the New Testament, with kurios being used to denote His authority over all creation (e.g., Philippians 2:11).

God the Father as "the God of Jesus"

While Jesus is worshipped as God, the New Testament also makes it clear that God the Father is above all in authority. Jesus refers to God the Father as His God, and the Scriptures maintain a distinction between the Father and the Son within the Trinity.

- John 20:17: "I ascend unto my Father, and your Father; and to my God, and your God."

- 1 Corinthians 11:3: "The head of Christ is God."

- Ephesians 1:17: "That the God of our Lord Jesus Christ, the Father of glory…"

This distinction is essential in understanding the Trinitarian relationship. While Jesus is fully God and equal to the Father in nature, the Father holds the ultimate authority in the Godhead. Thus, God the Father is described as the God of Jesus, not in a sense that diminishes Christ's divinity, but in a manner that reflects the relational roles within the Trinity.

Trinitarian Theology:

- Equality in Divinity: Father, Son, and Holy Spirit are co-equal in essence, yet they have distinct roles within the Godhead.

- Functional Subordination: Jesus submits to the Father in His earthly ministry and continues to recognize the Father as His God.

Strong's Concordance Analysis

- Lord (κυριός, kurios, Strong's G2962): Used by Thomas to affirm Jesus's divine authority. The word is equivalent to the Hebrew Adonai and is often used as a title for YHWH in the Old Testament.

- God (θεός, theos, Strong's G2316): A term used to describe Jesus by Thomas, recognizing His full divinity.

- Head (κεφαλή, kephalē, Strong's G2776): Used in 1 Corinthians 11:3 to describe the Father's authority over Christ, without denying the equality of their divine nature.

A Foundational Confession of Faith

Thomas's confession of Jesus as Lord and God remains a foundational statement of Christian belief. It reveals both the divine nature of Christ and the necessity of acknowledging Him as such for salvation. Thomas's journey from doubt to belief reflects the transformative power of encountering the risen Christ, and his confession serves as a model for all believers.

The absence of rebuke from Jesus in this instance, combined with the consistent New Testament witness to Jesus's divinity, leaves no doubt that Jesus is rightly called Lord and God. This truth is central to Christian theology, emphasizing that Jesus Christ is not merely a great teacher or prophet, but the eternal God who reigns over all.